20 EVENTS

Artists

WHO CREATED GREAT WORKS

CATHIE CUSH

RSVP

RAINTREE STECK-VAUGHN
PUBLISHERS
The Steck-Vaughn Company

Austin, Texas

Consultant: Roby McClellan, History Department, The Peddie School, Hightstown, New Jersey

**Developed for Steck-Vaughn Company by
Visual Education Corporation, Princeton, New Jersey**

Project Director: Jewel Moulthrop
Editor: Michael Gee
Copy Editor: Margaret P. Roeske
Editorial Assistants: Carol Ciaston, Stacy Tibbetts
Photo Research: Martin A. Levick
Production Supervisor: Maureen Ryan Pancza
Proofreading Management: William A. Murray
Word Processing: Cynthia C. Feldner
Interior Design: Maxson Crandall, Lee Grabarczyk
Cover Design: Maxson Crandall
Page Layout: Maxson Crandall, Lisa Evans-Skopas, Christine Osborne

Raintree Steck-Vaughn Publishers staff

Editor: Shirley Shalit
Project Manager: Joyce Spicer

Library of Congress Cataloging-in-Publication Data

Cush, Cathie, 1957–
    Artists who created great works / Cathie Cush.
        p.   cm. — (20 Events)
    Includes bibliographical references and index.
    ISBN 0-8114-4933-5
    1. Artists—Psychology—Juvenile literature.   2. Art—Themes, motives—Juvenile literature.   [1. Artists.   2. Art appreciation.]   I. Title.   II. Series.
N71.C87   1995
701′.1—dc20
                                                                94–14970
                                                                CIP
                                                                AC

Cover: Georgia O'Keeffe (inset) is shown in her studio against a background of one of her well-known flower paintings. This painting is called *Yellow Hickory Leaves with Daisy.*

Credits and Acknowledgments

Cover photos: Georgia O'Keeffe, 1887-1987, *Yellow Hickory Leaves with Daisy,* oil on canvas, 1928, 76 × 101.3 cm, Alfred Stieglitz Collection, gift of Georgia O'Keeffe, 1965.1180, photograph © 1994 The Art Institute of Chicago (background), "Georgia O'Keeffe," Copyright Amon Carter Museum, Fort Worth, Texas, Laura Gilpin Collection (inset)

Illustrations: Parrot Graphics, Precision Graphics

4: The Bettmann Archive; **5:** Superstock (left), Art Resource (right); **6:** Library of Congress; **7:** Art Resource (left), Art Resource (right); **8:** The Bettmann Archive (left), Art Resource (right); **9:** Superstock; **10:** Italian Government Travel Office; **11:** Art Resource (top), Art Resource (bottom); **12:** Bildarchiv Foto Marburg/Art Resource (top), Superstock (bottom); **13:** Superstock; **14:** British Tourist Authority; **15:** Syndication International; **16:** Prado/Art Resource; **17:** New York Public Library; **18:** Library of Congress (left), Superstock (right); **19:** Henry Lillie Pierce Fund/Museum of Fine Arts, Boston; **20:** Library of Congress; **21:** Erich Lessing/Art Resource; **22:** Philadelphia Museum of Art; **23:** Philadelphia Museum of Art (inset), Erich Lessing/Art Resource; **24:** Giraudon/Art Resource; **25:** Photo Researchers (left), Musée D'Orsay, Paris/Superstock (right); **26:** Hermitage, Leningrad/Art Resource; **27:** Dmitri Kessel/Life Magazine/Time Warner, Inc.; **28:** The Bettmann Archive; **29:** © 1994 The Museum of Modern Art, New York (top), Martin A. Levick (bottom); **30:** The Bettmann Archive; **31:** Schalkwijk/Art Resource; **32:** Rafael Macia/Photo Researchers; **33:** Guy Gillette/Photo Researchers; **34:** © 1994 The Art Institute of Chicago, All Rights Reserved (top), Courtesy Laura Gilpin Collection, Amon Carter Museum, Ft. Worth, Texas (bottom); **36:** Dan Budnik/Woodfin Camp; **37:** Tate Gallery, London/Art Resource (top), UNESCO/Michel Claude (bottom); **38:** Tom Dunham; **39:** Tate Gallery, London/Art Resource (top), Tony Howarth/Woodfin Camp (bottom); **40:** UPI/Bettmann; **41:** National Archives (left), Jimmy Carter Library (right); **42:** Superstock; **43:** The Bettmann Archive (top), Superstock (bottom)

Contents

Leonardo da Vinci

A late-15th-century artist and engineer, he embodied the idea of the Renaissance Man.

The Age of Discovery

Rebirth of Learning In the 15th century, Europe was undergoing a great change. This period is known as the Renaissance, from the French word for "rebirth." People began to look outward, beyond the security of their walled cities. Seafarers began to explore the horizon, returning with new goods and new ideas. Astrology—the belief that the stars and the planets determined people's lives—and alchemy—the belief that worthless metals could be turned into gold—gave way to the study of real sciences: astronomy, anatomy, chemistry, physics, and medicine. One man's name became most closely identified with the Renaissance. That man was Leonardo da Vinci.

Early Talent Leonardo was born near Florence, Italy, in 1452. By the age of 15, he was apprenticed to Andrea del Verrocchio, a well-known sculptor and painter. In this workshop, Leonardo learned metalwork, drawing, and painting. He began to practice different techniques. He worked on *chiaroscuro,* the use of light and shadow to show three-dimensional forms. He experimented with *sfumato,* a technique that blurs the edges of objects and colors to represent more closely what the eye really sees.

Leonardo da Vinci was interested in many different fields. He studied architecture, engineering, astronomy, anatomy, botany, and zoology.

The Renaissance Man

At about the age of 30, Leonardo left Florence for Milan, where he went to work for Duke Ludovico Sforza. The duke became his patron for the next 18 years.

The ability to do many things well was highly valued in this time of cultural rebirth. Leonardo's impressive variety of duties reflected his wide-ranging interests. As a civil and military engineer, he designed forts and canals. He also worked on developing new weapons and new spectacular effects for court pageants. Leonardo was a skilled musician and also served as the official artist in Sforza's court.

Leonardo's inquisitive mind never rested. He studied mathematics, physics, and anatomy. He drew natural objects, believing that art was a key to scientific understanding because artists were the best observers. His notebooks were full of extraordinary ideas well ahead of their time. They included the notion that the sun does not move and that humans might someday fly. He never published his writing, probably fearing the Roman Catholic Church's reaction to such revolutionary concepts.

Reality on Canvas Like others of his time, Leonardo often chose religious subjects for his paintings. But he represented them in a new way. His technical skill enabled him to make the human form more realistic than any painter before him had done. In so doing, he used several visual techniques. For instance, he painted objects smaller in the background to suggest distance. He grouped people in a pyramid, as in *The Virgin of the Rocks,* so that the viewer's eye went immediately to the main point of interest. This type of composition suggests order and timelessness. Da Vinci used strong lines and gestures to move the viewer's eye around the painting.

His famous painting of *The Last Supper* is particularly lifelike. In this work, Leonardo portrayed the emotions of shock, sorrow, disbelief, and suspicion among the apostles at the moment after Jesus announced that one of them would betray him. Sadly, this great mural no longer can be seen in its original splendor. When Leonardo painted it, he was experimenting with a new type of *fresco*—painting on wet plaster. He attempted to use oil paint on the wet plaster, and he found that the oil prevented the bonding that was possible when only water was used in the paint. The mural began to decay as early as 1517. Pinin Barcilon, an Italian, has been restoring this great work since 1979.

Mysterious Lady In 1499, after the French captured Milan, Leonardo left that city to seek work elsewhere. He served briefly as a mapmaker for adventurer Cesare Borgia, and then he returned to Florence. In 1503, he painted what may be the most famous painting in the world, *La Gioconda,* now known as the *Mona Lisa.* It is the portrait of the wife of a prominent Florentine banker. She sits calmly, with her hands quietly folded, before a mysterious landscape crossed by roads, bridges, and mountains that disappear into the mist. It is said that Francesco del Giocondo, who commissioned the portrait of his wife, disliked it and refused to pay for it. Leonardo eventually sold the painting, which now hangs in the Louvre in Paris, and which once was insured for $100 million.

This is a page from Leonardo's notebooks. He was more concerned with solving problems of structure and design than with constructing the building.

The Later Years

Genius at Work In his later years, Leonardo focused his energies on science and scientific illustration. He studied human anatomy by dissecting corpses. He analyzed the flight of insects and birds and studied ocean waves and currents. By 1513, he was almost entirely occupied by scientific research. Three years later, he went to France as architectural adviser to King Francis I.

Leonardo's Legacy Long before his death in 1519, Leonardo da Vinci was recognized as an artistic and scientific genius. Before him, artists had been considered mainly laborers and craftsmen. As he stated many times in his notes, the aim of his scientific studies was to make him a better painter. Leonardo succeeded. And in doing so, he raised art and artists to a higher level. The prestige of artists today rests on the first great gains of Leonardo and other masters of the Renaissance.

If it were sold today, this remarkable painting would probably bring more than $100 million at an auction. But the French government would never consider selling this extraordinary work.

Albrecht Dürer

This German printmaker
brought the ideals
of the Italian Renaissance
to northern Europe.

Troubled Times

Albrecht Dürer lived in Germany during a time of great religious and social upheaval. Many Catholics in northern Europe were unhappy with certain Church practices, such as the selling of indulgences, or pardons for sins. They also were unhappy with the rich life-style of many Church leaders.

The invention of the movable-type printing press enabled groups of discontented Catholics in Germany, Switzerland, and France to communicate easily with each other and exchange ideas. These groups wanted to reform the Church so that it conformed more closely to the teachings of the Bible. In fact, many people believed that the end of the world, as described in the biblical Book of Revelation, would occur during their lifetimes. They wanted to be spiritually ready for it.

In 1517, a German Catholic professor named Martin Luther compiled a list of 95 reasons for change within the Church. He posted his list on the door of All Saints Church in Wittenberg. This bold act marked the beginning of the religious movement known as the Protestant Reformation. Dürer, a passionately religious man, became a friend and follower of Luther.

Albrecht Dürer was
a deeply religious
man—a friend and
follower of Martin
Luther. Much of
his work had a
religious
theme.

▶ Dürer's subjects often were symbols of good and evil. In this engraving, the knight, a steadfast Christian soldier, is followed by his loyal dog and threatened by a grotesque horseman and a devil.

Between Two Worlds

Albrecht Dürer, the son of a goldsmith, worked in his father's shop and demonstrated an early talent for drawing. At the age of 15, he was apprenticed to a master painter and woodcut artist. There he learned various techniques for printmaking. Four years later, at the end of his apprenticeship, Dürer left his home in Nuremberg to learn copper engraving from the master of that art form, Martin Schongauer. However, that great engraver died just before Dürer arrived at his workshop. The young man continued his journey, which took him into Switzerland and eventually across the Alps into Italy.

The Best of Both Worlds Dürer found Italy to be much different from Germany. Here, in the south, it was sunny and warm. Furthermore, as a result of the fame and influence of such artists as Leonardo da Vinci and Michelangelo, artists in Italy were more highly respected than they were in the north. Their art was very different, too. The painting and sculpture of the Italian Renaissance had a feeling of balance and proportion that Dürer had not seen in the art of his homeland. He admired this discipline. Without it, he wrote, the ornate art style of Germany was like "a wild unpruned tree."

Dürer's own style blended ideas from both worlds. Like other northern European artists, he often portrayed medieval or biblical scenes. Knights, castles, devils, the Garden

A Strong Impression

Albrecht Dürer influenced artists throughout northern Europe. To appreciate his great skill, it is important to remember that woodcutting and engraving allow no room for error. The artist cannot erase or paint over a line that was made by mistake on the printing plate. Dürer's accuracy of detail was remarkable. Because he was so widely respected, people were receptive to his ideas about art and the role of the artist in society.

Dürer was one of the first artists to use himself as a frequent subject. In some of his self-portraits, it seems as if he deliberately painted himself to resemble Jesus.

In a time of religious unrest, Dürer brought to northern Europe the belief that artistic genius was inspired by God. With passion, intelligence, and enormous technical skill, Dürer brought the artistic ideals of the Italian Renaissance to much of Europe. He also bridged the gap between the Renaissance and the Middle Ages. He still is recognized as one of the greatest visual artists that Germany has ever produced.

This watercolor was so skillfully painted that one can see individual hairs on the animal's face.

of Eden, and the end of the world were the subjects of his paintings and engravings. His subjects were often symbols of good and evil, or reflections of the religious struggles and turmoil of the times. As with other art of that period, Dürer's engravings are rich with detail.

Part of Dürer's contribution to art was that disciplined approach to balance and proportion that he brought back to Germany. The figures in his pictures—people and animals—are carefully drawn in perfect proportion, much like the figures of Leonardo da Vinci. Dürer felt that it was his responsibility to teach this

attention to proportion to his fellow artists in the north. Toward the end of his life, he wrote many books and papers on his artistic theories.

From the Italians, Dürer also adopted the belief that an artist was more than just a craftsman. Creativity was as important as technical skill. Dürer explored many different areas in his work. In addition to his woodcuts and engravings, he gained recognition for his detailed watercolor studies of plants and animals in their natural settings. He also wrote papers on geometry, and he invented a device to show perspective, which was a forerunner of the camera.

Michelangelo Buonarroti

This Renaissance painter, sculptor, and architect is considered the most famous artist in history.

This sculpture, which is in St. Peter's Basilica in Rome, shows Mary mourning over the crucified body of Jesus. Michelangelo returned to this subject several times.

A Golden Age

In the late 1400s, under the rule of Lorenzo de Medici, Florence, Italy, thrived as a center for art and learning. Philosophers, poets, and painters gathered at the Medici palace. The palace was filled with Classical Greek and Roman statues and works by such early Renaissance artistic giants as Giotto, Masaccio, and Donatello. Florentine artists and intellectuals looked to the ancient philosopher Plato for many of their ideas. They believed that a person is a noble being, almost godlike, who should be celebrated. This view, popular with the ancient Greeks, had virtually disappeared with the coming of the Christian faith. The Greeks and Romans often portrayed soldiers and athletes in art. But for many centuries, artists had used religious themes for most of their subjects.

The Craft of Art In Florence, technical skills in the arts were held in high esteem. Under the guidance of older and experienced masters, young artists studied a variety of techniques. They practiced drawing. They learned how to paint on wet plaster to create frescoes. They were taught to model figures in wax or clay and to carve them from marble. They often studied literature and music as well. One of these young art students was Michelangelo Buonarroti.

This portrait of Michelangelo was painted by Giorgio Vasari, who was a student and a great admirer of the master painter, sculptor, and architect.

The Early Years

Michelangelo was born in Florence in 1475. At age 15, just two years after he had begun to study painting and sculpture, he was invited to stay at the palace of Lorenzo de Medici. Here he met many of the great artists and thinkers of the Renaissance. He was influenced by their belief in the nobility of humans.

Life from Stone Early in his career, Michelangelo showed an unusual talent for portraying the human form in his drawings and carvings. His special skill was in displaying its beauty and power in a way that went beyond just copying what he saw. He once said that sculpture was the process of "liberating the figure from the marble that imprisons it." His subjects truly seem to be alive.

Michelangelo was just 23 when he carved the *Pietà*, or Lamentation, at St. Peter's Basilica in Rome. This statue is of Mary mourning as she cradles the crucified body of Jesus. It demonstrates both Michelangelo's great technical skill and his intense religious feeling.

Another famous early work is the marble sculpture of *David.* The huge piece of marble, which eventually became the statue, had been in the cathedral in Florence for many years. But no one would risk carving it. According to legend, Michelangelo's father encouraged him to approach the city officials with a proposal for the statue. The proposal was accepted, and Michelangelo began to carve the 18-foot statue for the city when he was 26. He carved the Old Testament hero three times life size. The heroic body is turned slightly, as if trying to break free of the marble that contains it. Like the *Pietà,* this sculpture has timeless beauty and grandeur.

The Sistine Ceiling Although Michelangelo thought of himself mainly as a sculptor, he also is remembered for his painting. Most famous are his frescoes on the ceiling of the Sistine Chapel, the pope's private chapel in Rome. The Sistine Chapel was built in 1481. Several artists, including Sandro Botticelli, had painted its walls. In 1508, Pope Julius II asked Michelangelo to paint frescoes on the ceiling. The artist spent the next four years on the project. He had to lie on his back on a scaffold beneath the high ceiling. There he painted magnificent scenes from the Old Testament—from the Creation to the Flood. He carefully placed each scene so that it would fit within the ceiling's complicated arches. The figures he painted were inspired by the Bible. And they celebrate the beauty of the human form. The paintings have a sculptural solidity that influenced the styles of many other artists. Until recently, viewers thought that the scenes had been painted in dull colors. Cleaning the frescoes in the early 1980s revealed Michelangelo's original colors—which were bright.

Michelangelo had originally been called to Rome to work on the huge tomb of Pope Julius. The ceiling project interrupted that work, and he was able to do only part of it. He did complete his famous statue of *Moses,* though. He also finished sculptures of two slaves.

Changing World Then Michelangelo's world changed, and it showed in his art. In 1517, Martin Luther led a great religious revolution—the Protestant Reformation. This movement split the Christian religion into many different groups. This upheaval must have upset a deeply religious man like Michelangelo. Political turmoil occurred in the years that followed, too. Rome was attacked by Charles V of Spain, and the republic of Florence lost its independence. Michelangelo's work, such as *The Last Judgment,* became more serious and somber—a reflection of his feelings at the time.

Dome of St. Peter's Basilica
As Michelangelo reached his 60s, he spent most of his energy on architecture. He designed many buildings in Rome. In 1546, he was appointed chief architect for St. Peter's Basilica. His most visible contribution was the church's enormous ribbed dome. Today, it is a landmark in Rome. Its impressive design has been copied for such buildings as St. Paul's Cathedral in London and the Capitol in Washington, D.C.

Return to Roots Michelangelo lived a long and full life, working until his death at the age of 89. For one of his last sculptures, he returned to a subject that he had used for one of his first works: the Pietà. This later statue of the dead Christ is very different from his earlier version. The sad face of the old man who has just lowered the body of Christ from the cross could have been a portrait of the artist himself. Michelangelo damaged the sculpture in a fit of depression and never finished it.

In one of his last works, Michelangelo painted the Blessed and the Damned coming before God for the final judgment. The fresco, called *The Last Judgment,* occupies an entire wall in the Sistine Chapel. In this section, Mary and Jesus plead for God's mercy.

Gian Lorenzo Bernini

The influence of this Italian master dominated European sculpture for more than a century.

Changes in Attitude

The aim of many artists and architects of the Renaissance was to restore the city of Rome to its ancient glory. Sculptors chose classical heroes for the subjects of their work. In his design for St. Peter's Basilica, Michelangelo showed a Classical Greek cross shape for the building. Other works of the time demonstrated a similar sense of balance and proportion.

Religious Reformation During the last years of the Renaissance, religious rebellion occurred in Europe. Groups of Protestants grew strong in England, Germany, and France. In Spain and Italy, however, especially in Rome, the Catholic Church was able to remain strong. Religious and political leaders in Rome wanted the seat of the Catholic Church to be a place that inspired awe and religious devotion. A new style of art and design—one that emphasized drama, emotion, and religious fervor—was needed. Gian Lorenzo Bernini embodied that "Baroque" spirit.

Monumental Task

St. Peter's Basilica was still unfinished when Bernini came to Rome in 1605 at the age of seven. Following in his father's footsteps, Bernini became a sculptor. His early pieces resembled his father's work. But by the time he reached his 20s, Bernini developed a style that was truly his own. He portrayed his subjects in action. Whereas Michelangelo's statues are known for their remarkable restraint, Bernini's are full of energy and motion. Viewers are drawn into the action.

The facade, or front, of St. Peter's was completed in 1614. The interior, however, was still unfinished. In 1624, Bernini began work on the immense bronze canopy, called a baldachin, for the church's high altar. This elaborate structure, which is as tall as a ten-story building, took Bernini nine years to complete. Combining architecture and sculpture, the baldachin remains one of the finest examples of Baroque art ever created.

Many of Bernini's best-known works demonstrate his talent for combining several different art forms to

achieve the dramatic effect he sought. Behind the main altar, Bernini designed a second altar for the chair of St. Peter. He placed it in such a way that the sun streaming through a stained glass window makes the *Altar of the Chair* an awe-inspiring sight.

The Angel's Arrow In addition to his other interests, Bernini wrote plays. His love of the theater is evident in the drama of his artworks. One of his most vividly dramatic sculptures is *The Ecstasy of St. Theresa,* which is in a small chapel in the Roman church Santa Maria della Vittoria. For this remarkable work, Bernini combined marble and bronze, sculptural and architectural elements, painting and natural light to achieve emotional impact.

The scene is based on the writings of St. Theresa, a 16th-century nun who had mystical visions. Bernini's work shows an angel piercing St. Theresa's heart with the arrow of divine love. The expression on the saint's face is a mixture of intense pain and blissful happiness. The saint looks as if she is hovering over the altar on a cloud. Her robes seem to have a life of their own, as if they are being rippled by the wind. This high drama and intense feeling are the hallmarks of Baroque art.

A Life's Work In 1656, after completing *St. Theresa,* Bernini turned his attention to the exterior of St. Peter's Basilica. He had devoted much of his career to decorating its interior. The piazza, or plaza, in front of St. Peter's was his last great work.

Unlike Michelangelo's statue of David, which is known for its Classical beauty and restraint, Bernini's *David* is full of motion and feeling.

▲ This remarkable sculpture combines the great religious feeling and the ornate splendor of the Baroque period.

Beyond the Walls

Bernini worked on the interior and exterior of the basilica over the course of four decades. But this famous church is not the only place in Rome where he left his mark. A man of tremendous creative energy, Bernini built palaces and churches, including the oval-shaped Sant' Andrea al Quirinale. He designed fountains throughout the city. The largest and most impressive of these works is the *Fountain of the Four Rivers* in the Piazza Navona. Bernini was responsible for giving the city the Baroque flavor that it retains to this day.

Sharing the Vision Toward the end of his career, Bernini increasingly relied on assistants to carry out his designs. Among his helpers was Giovanni Battista Gaulli, whose ceiling for the Church of the Gesù in Rome clearly shows Bernini's influence.

Bernini's fame spread throughout Europe. In 1665, King Louis XIV of France invited him to Paris. Although the French court rejected his Baroque plans for the Louvre palace, they welcomed the artist warmly. Many architects adopted the ideas of this great Italian master. In this way, Bernini influenced European architecture for centuries.

Bernini designed an oval piazza framed by a colonnade, which is a series of columns supporting a roof. He chose this design to represent "the embracing arms of the church." By joining the great open space of the piazza with the basilica itself, Bernini made St. Peter's a doubly impressive structure.

▶ Unlike much of Bernini's other work, the design of the colonnade is simple—two facing rows of columns that suggest two gigantic arms extended in welcome.

Rembrandt van Rijn

This great 17th-century printmaker also was the most famous Dutch artist in history.

Unlike previous painters, Rembrandt portrayed Christ more as a human being than as a divine prince. He often used his neighbors as models.

Holland's Golden Age

The tiny region of Holland, now part of the Netherlands, was a major trade and cultural center in the 17th century. Ships from the Dutch East India and Dutch West India companies traded goods in Asia and North America. A solid Dutch middle class began to develop.

During this brief but glorious "golden age," the Dutch made very important contributions to navigation, exploration, commerce, and art. One of the most outstanding figures to emerge from this period was the painter and printmaker Rembrandt van Rijn.

The newly established middle class consisted of people who had money to spend on luxury items. One type of luxury item was art. People frequently commissioned, or hired, an artist to paint a specific subject—a portrait or a landscape, for example. A talented artist, such as Rembrandt, could earn a comfortable living by commissions—and Rembrandt did.

Artistic Truth

Rembrandt had a special talent for capturing the "soul" of his subjects. Many people compared him to the playwright William Shakespeare for his ability to portray different types of characters. The people he painted were not always handsome or beautiful. But he portrayed them with compassion and captured their humanity. The artistic truth was more important than the visible truth.

One example of Rembrandt's commitment to artistic integrity is in the story about his most famous painting, *The Night Watch*. In 1642, Rembrandt received a commission

Rembrandt was commissioned to paint a portrait of a military company. The painting, which is called *The Night Watch*, is unusual for its time because it shows the group in motion instead of posed.

1. A copper or zinc plate is heated and covered with ground (usually wax, resin, or pitch).

2. The artist draws on the surface with an etching needle.

3. The entire plate is immersed in an acid bath. Acid eats into the cut lines but does not affect the metal still covered by ground.

4. The plate is removed from the acid. The etching ground is removed, leaving the lines eaten into the grooves

5. The plate is covered with ink. Surface ink is wiped off. Ink stays only in the etched grooves.

6. The plate is covered with a moist sheet and run through a printing press.

Like engraving, etching requires great drawing skill because, once a line is made, it cannot be painted over or erased.

for a group portrait of a military company. Instead of a posed portrait in a room, as was customary, Rembrandt painted the group in motion. As a result, some of the figures are in shadow, and some are partially hidden by overlapping. Although each member of the company had contributed equally to the artist's fee, they did not receive equal treatment.

Biblical Scenes Rembrandt's concept of artistic honesty extended to the Old Testament scenes that he painted and etched. For his etching, Rembrandt experimented with a new technique that involved scratching wax on a copper plate. In an etching, the copper plate is covered with an acid-resistant material, such as wax. Lines are scratched in the wax, exposing the copper plate. The plate is dipped in acid, which "etches" the lines that will eventually hold the ink. This method enabled him to achieve finer lines and more subtle effects than engraving directly on copper.

Before Rembrandt, most Christian artists painted God, angels, saints, and the Holy Family. Rembrandt's religious scenes focused on people and their relationship to God. Even when Rembrandt depicted Jesus Christ, the artist showed him as a gentle teacher rather than a divine prince. For a time, Rembrandt lived in the Jewish section of Amsterdam. He often used his Jewish neighbors as models for his religious works. To achieve authenticity, he had his models dress in Near Eastern clothing that he had collected.

A Dark Period Rembrandt's work became more somber and reflective following the early death of his wife, Saskia, in 1642. Over the next decade, the number of commissions he received declined. But his career was not over. He was married again—to an art dealer—and continued to receive many important commissions.

Throughout his life, Rembrandt painted many portraits of himself. The 50 self-portraits that remain show the artist's development from confident youth to wise old master. Never did he try to make himself more handsome than he was. But in each painting, he is fully human.

Inspiration and Imitation

At the height of his career, Rembrandt had a large studio and school where he trained young artists. About 20 of his students became great artists in their own right—and the cause of some confusion.

At one time, the paintings attributed to Rembrandt numbered more than 1,000. By the late 1960s, art historians determined that Rembrandt probably painted fewer than 400 of those works. The rest were done by his apprentices. Museum officials and collectors were shocked to learn that some of the paintings—for which they had paid millions—were not genuine "Rembrandts," and were worth a good deal less than they had paid.

The controversy has stirred the art world for more than two decades, and the debate continues. Members of the Rembrandt Research Project in the Netherlands are still examining works throughout the world to determine if, in fact, they were painted by the great master himself.

Rembrandt's first wife, Saskia, frequently modeled for him. She is pictured here in *Saskia with the Red Flower.*

13

Christopher Wren

This English architect and designer helped to rebuild London after the Great Fire of 1666.

The facade of St. Paul's Cathedral is unusual because of its two stories of paired columns.

"Renaissance Man"

Although the Italian Renaissance ended before Christopher Wren was born in 1632, the ideal of the well-rounded individual was still highly valued. By the 17th century, it was not uncommon for men trained in one field to pursue other fields as well. Often, these highly educated men made important contributions in areas outside their primary specialties. Christopher Wren was such a man.

Wren had a thorough education in the sciences. By the time he was 30, he had been named the Saville Professor of Astronomy at Oxford University in England—a very important honor. However, he is remembered not as an astronomer but as an architect.

While at Oxford, Wren designed the buildings for the university's Trinity College. In 1665, he traveled to France, where he came to love the French style of architecture. Wren returned to England in 1666. That year, disaster struck the city of London.

Disaster Brings Opportunity

By the mid-1600s, London was a busy commercial center with narrow, twisting streets crowded with old wooden buildings. When a major fire broke out in September 1666, it consumed most of the city. Christopher Wren drew up a plan for rebuilding London. The plan was considered impractical by those who were in a hurry to restore the city. Although his plan was rejected, Wren still made his mark on the project.

A New Landmark

In 1669, Wren was named Surveyor of His Majesty's Works and was appointed to many building commissions. These positions put him in charge of designing and constructing many public buildings in London, especially in the financial district known as the City. As the king's surveyor, Wren supervised the construction of more than 50 churches and designed St. Paul's Cathedral—probably his most famous work.

> "Below is laid the builder of this Church and City,
> Christopher Wren,
> Who lived for more than ninety years,
> Not for himself alone but for the public good.
> Reader, if you seek his monument,
> Look around you."
>
> —on Wren's tomb in St. Paul's
> translated from Latin

The fire that destroyed most of London in 1666 gave Christopher Wren, a young astronomy professor, an opportunity to work in his adopted profession—architecture. By the end of his career, Wren had designed and built more than 50 churches and other buildings.

The original cathedral was a medieval structure that was shaky even before the Great Fire. Further damaged by the blaze, it had to be replaced. Wren envisioned a structure on the scale of St. Peter's Basilica in Rome. After all, he reasoned, a cathedral should represent strength and stability if the people were to have faith in the Anglican Church, which was less than 100 years old. Wren worked on several plans before submitting the design that was eventually accepted in 1675. The design called for a Latin cross-shaped floor plan—in which one arm of the cross is longer than the other—and a large dome flanked by elaborate bell towers.

The foundation stone for the cathedral was laid in June 1675. Wren worked on the cathedral until its completion 35 years later.

Thinking Big Built mostly of limestone blocks, St. Paul's is 555 feet long—almost large enough for two football fields. The west entrance, with its stately double columns, is 180 feet wide. The outside walls are 111 feet high. The dome, which is 336 feet high, was modeled after the dome of St. Peter's Basilica (the largest dome in the world). The dome of St. Paul's is the second tallest.

Wren was influenced by many styles, including Italian Renaissance and French Baroque, when he designed St. Paul's. In his design, he combined elements of these styles to form a structure that is solid, solemn, and impressive. The British Parliament declared St. Paul's Cathedral complete in 1711. Christopher Wren was 78 years old.

Inspiring Spires

Completion of the cathedral marked the end of Wren's architectural career. He fell out of favor and lost his position as Royal Surveyor. When he died in 1723, he was buried in a simple tomb in the crypt of St. Paul's.

Despite the disfavor Wren endured in his last years, he left a magnificent legacy. For almost three centuries, the tall spires on Wren's churches delineated the London skyline. Many were destroyed during the air raids of World War II, but many were left unscarred. Some of the damaged ones have been restored. Amazingly, St. Paul's Cathedral was spared during the German bombing of the city, even though it was a massive target.

Christopher Wren's refined architectural style was copied by generations of European architects. Those who followed him would further modify the style to reflect the changing tastes of the growing middle class in Europe.

In designing the interior of St. Paul's, Wren emphasized the elements of arches, frames, and circles.

Francisco Goya

This Spanish painter
and printmaker
used his art
for social commentary.

The Early Years

In 1746, Francisco Goya was born into a Spanish peasant family. Even though Goya eventually found himself in the royal court, he never lost his sympathy for the struggles of poor people. He was one of the first painters to express his social views and feelings in his work.

In 1774, Goya came to Madrid where he sold drawings to the royal tapestry maker. He often portrayed the activities of the Spanish upper classes, using light and shadow in the same manner as Rembrandt van Rijn and another Spanish painter, Diego Velázquez. In 1786, Goya was appointed court painter to King Charles III.

In 1800, Goya painted his famous portrait of *The Family of Charles IV.* The royal family was less than perfect, and Goya painted what he saw. The king was weak and not very intelligent; his wife was unattractive and unfaithful to the king. Art critics have long maintained that the royal family was not smart enough to realize that the painter was making fun of them. Many people thought that such "realism" was, in this case, cruel and disrespectful.

New Hope

Even though Goya moved among the Spanish nobility, he had no sympathy for the upper class. He thought it unfair that a few very wealthy people ruled over the great masses of poor people. The nobles were corrupt and greedy, and they cared little for the rights of the peasants. In this way, they resembled the upper class in France, which had been overthrown during the French Revolution in 1789. The new French government, under Emperor Napoléon I, was founded on the idea that the people should hold the power. As Napoléon expanded his influence, Goya and other Spanish intellectuals hoped that the French ruler would bring positive change to Spain.

Hopes Dashed In 1808, Napoléon invaded Spain. Many Spaniards resented the French occupation, believing that the French were no better than the Spanish nobles. Civil war erupted in Spain between small

In *The Third of May,* Goya depicted the savage behavior of the French troops that occupied his homeland.

ARTISTS WHO USED SOCIAL/POLITICAL THEMES IN THEIR WORKS

Artist	Work	Theme
Jacques-Louis David	*The Death of Marat* (1793)	Shows the assassination of an important leader of the French Revolution
Théodore Géricault	*Raft of the Medusa* (1819)	A political scandal in which passengers on a French ship were set adrift
Eugène Delacroix	*Massacre at Chios* (1824)	Depicts the plight of Greeks in their fight for independence from the Turks
Honoré Daumier	*Rue Transnonain* (1834)	Protests the murder of a group of workers
Édouard Manet	*The Execution of the Emperor Maximilian of Mexico* (1867)	Depicts the assassination of a popular leader
Diego Rivera	Frescoes at the Ministry of Education Building in Mexico City (1923–1928)	Promoted social and economic reform
José Clemente Orozco	*Hispano-America* (1930)	Shows support of the peasants and workers during the Mexican Revolution
Pablo Picasso	*Guernica* (1937)	Protest against the bombing of a Spanish town by Germans
Maya Yang Lin	Vietnam War Memorial, Washington, D.C. (1982)	Memorial to Americans who died during the Vietnam War

Many artists depicted the brutality of war and the hypocrisy of society. This list names a few and their famous works.

bands of fighters known as *guerrillas,* from the Spanish word for "little war." In May 1808, when Napoléon had his brother Joseph crowned king of Spain, the fighting became particularly savage on both sides. Goya's painting *The Third of May* captures the tragedy of the times.

Antiwar Protest Completed in 1814, the painting shows the execution of Madrid citizens by a French firing squad. They are being shot for an uprising that occurred the day before. Goya portrayed the helpless victims in three groups: the bloody corpses on the ground, the men about to be shot gesturing wildly in protest and terror, and the men shielding their eyes from the horror before them. The artist depicted the executioners as an impersonal, faceless killing machine. It was as if Goya had looked into the future of warfare to a time when soldiers dropped bombs

without ever seeing the people they killed. *The Third of May* is an early example of social protest in art.

Throughout his career, Goya protested war and the brutality he saw around him. A series of etchings called *The Disasters of War* depicts scenes of a country torn apart by war. Although the country is Spain, the human suffering is universal.

An Era of Emotion

To avoid persecution for the outspoken views expressed in his work, Goya left the country in 1824. He lived the last four years of his life in voluntary exile in France.

Goya had many friends and admirers in France, including several painters and writers. Many elements in Goya's work were a preview of the styles that became popular in the 19th century. For example, the Romantics would focus on the same kind of individual and mass suffering that Goya portrayed. Much later, the strange and dreamlike elements of some of Goya's etchings would reappear in the 20th century in the Surrealist art of painters such as Salvador Dali.

Francisco Goya expressed his own beliefs through his images. He portrayed his subjects as he saw them, combining realistic detail with his own interpretation of their character. By doing so, he was one of the first visual artists to use his work for social commentary.

Goya produced a series of satirical paintings and prints in which he criticized human vanity and vice. He called them *Los Caprichos,* which suggests irresponsible behavior. In this drawing, Goya depicts someone he knew as a silly animal.

Joseph M. W. Turner

This English landscape painter glorified the awesome power of nature.

Turner once believed that nature was all-powerful. By the time he painted *Rain, Steam, and Speed* (shown here), he had accepted the triumph of humans over the forces of nature.

Turner was fascinated by the forces of nature. He once had himself tied to the mast of a ship during a storm so that he could experience the full force of the wind and water swirling around him.

The Age of Reason

By the 1700s, people were looking at the world in new ways. Sir Isaac Newton and other scientists had made rapid and great advances in mathematics, physics, and astronomy. Each day seemed to bring new knowledge about the universe.

Still shaken by the religious turbulence of the Protestant Reformation, Europeans began to put their faith in science. They believed that they could control nature through science. They also believed that human reason and understanding were the keys to a better world.

Industrial Revolution With knowledge came a host of new inventions that changed daily life throughout Europe. Industries grew and factories sprang up in the cities of Europe. Great masses of people left the farms to work in the urban factories. The world entered the Industrial Revolution, a time in which methods of farming, production, and transportation changed dramatically.

Romantic Counterrevolution Not everyone welcomed the blossoming of science and technology. A literary, musical, and artistic movement called Romanticism opposed the triumphs of technology. The Romantics rebelled against the idea that human beings are rational creatures and that human intelligence can control nature. Instead, they saw nature as the most powerful force shaping the world. The Romantics believed that those who put their faith in science had lost their souls. One of the painters who glorified nature in this way was Joseph Mallord William Turner.

Color, Light, and Power

Born in 1775, Joseph Turner was a talented child who began his formal study of art at the Royal Academy of Arts in London while he was in his teens. Working first in watercolor and later in oils, he painted a wide variety of outdoor subjects. He is best known for seascapes and landscapes that show the awesome and dramatic power of nature. Each year, Turner made a trip through England or the European continent to make preliminary sketches for his paintings.

Before Turner, landscape painting was regarded as less serious than other art forms. Most landscapes were merely pretty pictures. But Turner believed that they should reflect human feelings and struggles. To him, a painting's overall impact was more important than its small details.

Back to Nature Turner often portrayed disasters, such as a fire or a storm, emphasizing the force of nature overpowering technology. One such painting is *Steamer in a Snowstorm.* In it, Turner shows a steamship—a relatively new invention at that time—being overwhelmed by the wind and raging sea.

Turner cared little for realistic detail. The dark hull in the painting is enough to let the viewer know that it is a ship. Turner focused his energy on conveying the "feel" of the wind, the waves, and the dark storm clouds.

Eventually, Turner recognized that change was inevitable. In *Rain, Steam, and Speed,* a steam-powered locomotive emerges from the rain and fog. Not even the storm can stop it. Change was coming, Turner seemed to say, though it might not be an improvement.

Similarly, in *The Fighting Téméraire,* a great white ghost of a sailing ship is being retired. The dignified vessel is being towed through the harbor by a dirty, little, smoke-spewing tugboat. It is easy to see that Turner preferred the old, wind-driven craft.

"Airy Visions"

John Constable, another English landscape painter and a contemporary of Turner's, said that Turner's works were "airy visions, painted with tinted steam." Other artists had discovered the power of intense color and light, but Turner was the first to make color and light more important than detail. A dark shadow could suggest a ship and a batch of orange, yellow, and red could convey fire without showing individual flames. In later years, the Impressionists would expand on Turner's idea of using light and color to convey moods and merely suggest details.

When Turner died in 1851, he left behind a large body of work—nearly 300 oil paintings and 19,000 drawings and watercolors. These works were cataloged by British art critic John Ruskin. In 1987, a new addition to London's Tate Gallery opened. This new building was devoted entirely to the work of Joseph M. W. Turner.

The Slave Ship depicts an incident that Turner had read about. When an epidemic broke out on a slave ship, the captain threw the slaves overboard. He did this because he was insured against the loss of his cargo but not against disease.

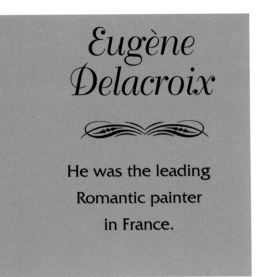

Eugène Delacroix

He was the leading
Romantic painter
in France.

Classical or Expressive

In the years following the reign of King Louis XIV, who ruled France from 1643 to 1715, Paris became an important center for the arts. As a result, many artists came there to study. In the late 18th century, some painters came to learn from Jacques-Louis David, the great Neoclassical master. *Neoclassical* refers to a revival of the Classical ideals of balance, serenity, and judgment. David emphasized discipline and drawing technique.

Elsewhere in Europe, however, many artists were breaking away from the Classical style. They wanted to express their feelings through their work. By the early 1800s, Francisco Goya in Spain was painting intensely emotional antiwar scenes. In England, Joseph M. W. Turner portrayed the power of nature as it overshadowed the machines of humans. Poets, too, chose emotional themes for their work. It was this expressive approach to art that influenced Eugène Delacroix.

Romance over Reason

Born in 1798, Delacroix adopted the ideals of the artists, writers, and intellectuals known as the Romantics. They believed that experience and emotion were more powerful than reason and restraint. They were fascinated by the darker, more dramatic side of life.

By the time Delacroix was 25, he already had established his reputation as a Romantic painter. People considered his early works shocking—scenes of emotional and physical violence. He cared little for the clean lines and controlled drawing techniques of David and his student Jean Auguste Dominique Ingres. Instead, he used broad brush strokes and bold color. His paintings were full of action and drama; several were inspired by war.

Like other Romantics of his time, Delacroix's sympathies were with the Greeks in their war for independence against the Turks. Their struggle for freedom symbolized the personal liberty that the Romantics so strongly believed in.

Massacre at Chios shows the painter's outrage at the oppression of the Greeks. In this painting, Delacroix captured the viewer's sympathy by showing a particularly poignant image of Greek families awaiting death or slavery at the hands of the Turks.

Another painting—*Liberty Leading the People*—is perhaps the most famous visual image of revolution ever painted. In this painting, Liberty, brandishing both flag and bayonet, leads Parisians over the dead bodies of citizens and royal troops to the barricades during the French Revolution.

Life's Adventure Like the Romantic poet Lord Byron, Eugène Delacroix was an adventurer. In 1832, he traveled to Morocco and Algeria. There he saw an exotic world of brilliant color and fantastical scenes. He carefully recorded his observations in his *Journals*. His travels sparked his rich imagination. His paintings, after the North African journey, often depicted combat—between beasts and between men and beasts. *The Lion Hunt* is typical of this period.

Literature also inspired Delacroix. One of Shakespeare's great tragedies was the inspiration for *Hamlet and Horatio in the Graveyard*. In this painting, the figures stand, under a blood-red sky, surrounded by reminders of their mortality.

Taking Sides "But skies are not red," some critics said. The art world was split between those who preferred the Classicism of Ingres and those who supported Delacroix's bold new vision. For more than 25

Delacroix began his career as a Romantic painter, but he soon developed an innovative style that anticipated the Impressionists who followed him.

Periods of Romanticism often develop as a reaction against the restraint of Classicism.

years, these two painters remained professional rivals—on opposite sides of the issue. French newspapers covered their "war of styles" with enthusiasm. This lively debate earned France a reputation as the world capital of artistic ideas. Although Ingres initially won most of the honors, Delacroix eventually won many prizes, including the prestigious Legion of Honor medal.

COMPARISON OF CLASSICAL AND ROMANTIC ART

Classical Art	Romantic Art
Emphasizes reason and logic over feelings	Emphasizes the importance of feelings in understanding the world
Stresses order, balance, and symmetry	Stresses imagination
Values moderation of emotional expression	Encourages spontaneous and full expression of feelings
Expresses established ideas	Rebels against social customs and artistic traditions
Follows strict rules, standards, and traditions	Includes a variety of styles due to absence of rules

In 1832, Delacroix visited North Africa. He was fascinated by what he saw there. The numerous sketches he made at the time provided him with a wealth of subject matter for his later work. One of these—*The Lion Hunt*—is shown here.

A New Twist

Throughout his career, Delacroix kept journals, which became important works on color theory. He noticed that pure colors were as rare in nature as straight lines. He once wrote that "when the tones [degrees of color] are right, the lines draw themselves."

Toward the end of Delacroix's career, the debate in the art world took a new turn. French painter Gustave Courbet questioned why Neoclassicists looked to the past and Romantics looked inward for their inspiration. Courbet felt that artists should draw inspiration from the world around them. His new style, called Realism, together with Delacroix's color theories, paved the way for the Impressionists of the late 19th century.

In his lifetime, Eugène Delacroix brought bold color to Romantic painting. He is now regarded as the best representative of that style. With other Romantics, such as writer Victor Hugo and composer Hector Berlioz (both French), he broke the rules of rationalism and reflected deep emotions.

Auguste Rodin

This controversial French sculptor revived a disappearing art and freed sculpture from the Classical tradition.

CASTING A BRONZE USING THE LOST WAX METHOD

1. A core of plaster or clay is surrounded by a layer of wax.
2. The wax is shaped as the sculpture is going to look. The wax must be the same thickness as the final bronze is to be.
3. Hollow wax rods are applied to the surface of the figure, to act as drainpipes.
4. The figure is covered with an outer plaster coat and heated.
5. The wax runs out, bronze is poured in. When the bronze hardens, the outer cover is removed.
6. The drainpipes are broken off. The interior core of the plaster or clay is broken up and shaken out. The sculpture is ready to be polished.

The steps outlined here are for large pieces. For small pieces, a simpler method—called solid cast—is used.

Classical Sculpture

At the age of 14, Auguste Rodin enrolled in art school. He intended to study sculpture and decorative arts. These two art forms had changed little in the two centuries since Gian Lorenzo Bernini left his ornate Baroque touch on the churches and fountains of Rome in the 1600s. Sculptors of public monuments still showed Classical heroes with perfect bodies.

Unlike painters of the mid-1800s, most sculptors of the time did not question tradition. Rodin was the exception.

Break with Tradition Rodin studied anatomy and worked as an apprentice. He earned money by carving ornamental details for established sculptors. In his spare time, he pursued his own projects. In 1864, when Rodin was just 24, he unveiled the first of many innovative sculptures. He called the work *The Man with the Broken Nose.* The critics called it rough and unfinished. Many sculptors made small models of their work for study, as painters made preliminary sketches before applying paint to canvas. But these models usually were for the artist's private use, not for public display. Rodin was the first to use the "unfinished" as an artistic statement. He believed that it was up to the artist to decide when a work was "finished."

Rodin was concerned with body movement. He made quick sketches of his models to refer to later. Before casting his sculptures in bronze, he modeled them in plaster or clay.

A New Role for Models

Rodin admired the sculptures of Michelangelo and Donatello, which he had seen during a trip to Italy. But he disliked the strict approach that Classical sculpture had taken since the Renaissance. Rodin wanted his work to be natural, realistic, and emotional—not only decorative.

Cast in Bronze Rodin exhibited a major work, *The Age of Bronze,* in 1877. It is a statue of a young nude male stretching as if he is just awakening. It is so lifelike that some people thought that Rodin had made a plaster cast of a live model. In reality, Rodin had modeled the statue from clay, paying careful attention to anatomical detail. Then he had made a plaster mold of the clay model. Next he had cast it—filled the plaster mold with bronze—to create the statue. When he removed the plaster mold, the bronze statue remained. Sometimes, more than one statue was cast from a mold.

A New Master Rodin was considered a master in his own lifetime. He had many apprentices working in his studio. One of them, Camille Claudel, became an important artist in her own right.

Rodin received many important commissions. He rarely turned down

Rodin made many rough sketches, such as this one *(left),* for his statue of Balzac. Bronze casting enables more than one statue to be made from the same mold. This statue of Balzac is in Paris; another casting is in the Museum of Modern Art in New York City.

interesting work, even if he was too busy to do it. In 1880, the French government asked Rodin to design a new entrance for the Museum of Decorative Arts. The project occupied him for the rest of his life, though it never was completed. Called *The Gates of Hell,* the design was inspired by the *Inferno,* a part of the epic poem *The Divine Comedy* written by Italian poet Dante Alighieri. Rodin had always been interested in figures in motion. He often asked his models to move randomly around the studio. When he spotted an unusual position, he would ask the model to hold it. He would then make a quick sketch. Many of the unusual poses in *The Gates of Hell* were achieved in this manner.

Burghers and Balzac Other commissions took Rodin's attention away from the project. In 1884, the town of Calais, France, asked Rodin for a statue to commemorate the extraordinary bravery of several citizens during the Hundred Years War. Rodin's

The Burghers of Calais depicts the six men who volunteered to sacrifice their lives to the English king in return for the town's safety. Rodin showed the figures walking into the English camp with nooses around their necks. Some look despairing, others look defiant. Rodin wanted the sculpture to sit at ground level so that viewers could be a part of the scene.

The Burghers of Calais was not the glorious, upbeat monument that the town leaders had expected. For seven years, they argued about it. When it was finally displayed in 1895, it stood on a pedestal.

Rodin's monument to French novelist Honoré de Balzac was rejected as "an ignoble and insane nightmare" by the Writers Association that had commissioned the work in 1891. The ten-foot statue shows a disheveled writer striding in his dressing gown. The association thought that it was unflattering. Rodin felt that he had captured Balzac's spirit and refused to change it. The statue never was cast during the sculptor's lifetime.

Beast or Beauty?
Art critics debated Rodin's work throughout the sculptor's career. Many recognized his genius. Rodin gained popularity on both sides of the Atlantic. In 1911, the British government purchased a duplicate casting of *The Burghers of Calais* for the Houses of Parliament. The following year, the Metropolitan Museum of Art in New York City opened the Rodin Room.

Legacy in Bronze Before Rodin died in 1917, he bequeathed all his molds to the Musée Rodin in Paris. Some never had been cast. Among these molds was the plaster mold for *The Gates of Hell.* In the 1920s, a wealthy American filmmaker, Jules Mastbaum, arranged to have this and several other works cast. With these pieces, Mastbaum established a Rodin Museum in Philadelphia, Pennsylvania.

These collections have enabled many Americans and tourists to see and appreciate the works of the man who breathed new life into sculpture. By freeing sculpture from the traditions of the past, Rodin showed the world that this art form, like painting, could change to reflect the changing times.

23

Claude Monet

His career as a painter spanned more than 50 years and his name became synonymous with Impressionism.

The End of Romanticism

New Techniques In response to the machines that were taking over 19th-century Europe, the Romantic artists turned toward imagination and emotion. They were trying to escape from the dreariness around them. But in the 1850s, new schools of artistic thought rose to challenge the way in which Romantics depicted the world. Painters such as Gustave Courbet portrayed the world in a realistic, not an emotional way. Another group, as yet unnamed, began to experiment with new painting techniques and new ways of viewing the world.

Enter the Camera One of the events that drove this new group of artists was the invention of the camera. The first commercial camera was developed in France in 1839. That same year, Louis Daguerre invented a photographic process known as *daguerreotype*.

The camera, and the accompanying scientific analysis of light and color, led a group of artists to think more about *how* and *what* we see. For example, when we glance across a river and see a bush, we do not see individual leaves and twigs. We get an impression of a patch of green, which we know from experience has leaves and twigs.

Impression: Sunrise (shown here) gave the movement its name. There are no clear outlines, and nothing in the painting is solid. It is the recording of a fleeting moment of visual experience.

The Start of Impressionism

French painter Édouard Manet was one of those artists who tried to paint the world in a new way. Manet used lights and darks in an almost photographic way—illuminating his figures as a flashbulb might.

Manet influenced many young artists of his day, including another Frenchman, Claude Monet. By the end of his career, Monet would push Manet's techniques to the extreme.

"Slapdash" Art In 1874, a group of artists gave a show in a photographer's studio. The group included Claude Monet, Paul Cézanne, Edgar Degas, and Auguste Renoir. They held their exhibit there because no art gallery in France would display their work.

One of the paintings in the show was Monet's *Impression: Sunrise.* It shows a harbor on a misty morning. Monet used only color to create a composition. There are no outlines; nothing in the painting is clear-cut or solid. It is an attempt to catch a fleeting moment—moments later, the sun would be in another place, the small boat would have moved, all would look different.

One hostile critic, Louis Leroy, said that this and other paintings in the show looked unfinished and "slapdash," and he called the artists "impressionists." But, instead of being insulted, the group adopted the name as a banner and used it to describe their new style.

Points of Light The Impressionists painted landscapes, seascapes, and cityscapes using splashes of pure, unmixed color. They relied on the viewer's eye to "mix" it. The Impressionists broke with the tradition of painting their subjects with pinpoint accuracy. Shapes were only

In 1883, Monet settled in Giverny in northern France. There he cultivated a garden and built the water-lily pond that inspired much of his later work.

In Different Directions

As one looks at the Impressionists' work today, it is difficult to imagine the outrage these paintings caused when they were first shown. These painters, who blurred details in swirls of color and light, were neither slapdash nor careless. They created and perfected a revolutionary style of painting. Still the subjects are recognizable.

Commercial success in the 1880s gave Monet the freedom to paint what he wanted. Monet continued to experiment with Impressionism throughout his long career. Many other Impressionists did not. By the 1880s, the group had begun to fall apart. Each artist took a different direction. Renoir abandoned Impressionism because he felt that he was forgetting how to draw. Cézanne returned to the Classic ideals of balance and composition. Vincent van Gogh, who went through an Impressionist phase, gave it up because to him it lacked emotion.

Still, these artists had a major impact on the history of art. Their free brush strokes and use of bright colors influenced the development of modern art. In the 20th century, painters would increasingly emphasize visual impact over recognizable subject matter.

suggested; lines marking the side of a house or the edge of a leaf were blurred. Instead, specks of color—when viewed from a distance—conveyed the overall form of what they painted. The purpose was to catch just a glimpse of a particular moment in time.

The development of chemical pigments gave artists a wide range of colors. Previously, paints had been made of natural substances. With the new pigments, artists experimented with color. Monet almost never used black or brown, even when he painted shadows or dark objects. For example, for the locomotive in his painting of *La Gare Saint-Lazare* in Paris, Monet used dark blue with traces of other colors.

Changing Light The Impressionists worked outdoors and painted directly from nature. They had to work quickly, before the light changed. That left little time to worry about fine detail. But it allowed them to see the same object in different ways. Monet often painted a series of paintings of the same subject to show these different appearances as the light changed.

A story is told that one day Monet came upon two haystacks and began to paint them. Within 15 minutes, the light had changed, and the haystacks looked different. Monet reached for a second canvas and began another picture of the haystacks. A few minutes later, he sent for more canvases. Monet paid the farmer to leave the haystacks in the field through the winter so that he could paint them in different seasons as well as at different times of the day.

Monet painted about 30 different views of the cathedral at Rouen. He also painted many different versions of the water lilies in the pond at his home in Giverny.

This version of Monet's famous water lilies is called *The Water Lily Pond*. It is exhibited in the Musée D'Orsay in Paris.

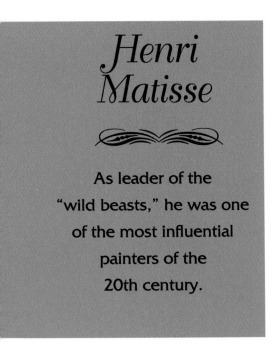

Henri Matisse

As leader of the "wild beasts," he was one of the most influential painters of the 20th century.

The Pace of Change

The changes in thought, culture, and artistic expression that made up the Renaissance occurred over several centuries. Even after the Renaissance, the influence of one style of painting or another might last a century. But as time passed, ideas and customs changed more rapidly. After the Industrial Revolution in the late 1700s and early 1800s, each generation seemed to have a new way of looking at life and art.

Market Driven Change came quickly because, as the market for art expanded, artists were able to experiment with new styles. Individuals—not just institutions, such as churches, museums, and governments—had money to spend on painting and sculpture. Art collectors had different likes and dislikes. They bought art that suited their individual tastes. Newspapers regularly carried news about artists and their exhibits. One group of artists that made headlines was led by French painter Henri Matisse.

A Get-Well Gift Matisse came to art relatively late in life. As a young man, he worked as a law clerk and took some drawing classes in his spare time. When he was 20, his mother gave him some oil paints to occupy him while he was recovering from appendicitis. Matisse enjoyed painting so much that he tried to persuade his father, a grain merchant, to allow him to study art professionally.

After two years of arguments, Matisse's father let him enroll in the Académie Julien in Paris. By 1895, Henri Matisse was studying in the studio of Gustave Moreau at the École des Beaux-Arts (School of Fine Arts)—the official art school of the Académie. Matisse's studies gave him a solid background in the traditional artistic theories, including color and composition. He learned to copy the paintings of past masters that hung in the famous Louvre museum in Paris.

Eventually, he rebelled against the school's traditional approach, as he came to know the new styles of Moreau and the increasingly popular artists of the time, such as Paul Cézanne, Vincent van Gogh, and Paul Gauguin. Soon, Matisse began to develop a style all his own.

The Wild Beasts

A New Style In 1905, Matisse unveiled his shocking new style. He and a group of friends had an exhibit. The show outraged the Parisian art community. Matisse and the others whose work was on display had used bold colors in a striking new way. Matisse had painted a portrait of his wife, using red-orange and violet on a green background. Matisse later explained that he had chosen these colors for their emotional effect.

The exhibit included a single Renaissance-style statue surrounded by these new-style paintings of Matisse and the others. One journalist wrote that the statue was "*Donatello au milieu des fauves,*" which means "Donatello among the wild beasts." (Donatello was a great 15th-century sculptor.) Instead of taking offense, Matisse and his friends adopted the name and proudly began to call themselves *Fauves.* Other well-known Fauves include Georges Rouault, Raoul Dufy, and Georges Braque.

In *Harmony in Red,* the room is flooded with bright color that encourages the viewer to share the artist's enthusiasm for the visual experience.

> "*What I am after, above all, is expression. . . . I am unable to distinguish between the feeling I have for life and my way of expressing it. . . . The whole arrangement of my picture is expressive. The placement of figures or objects, the empty spaces around them, the proportions—everything plays a part.*"
>
> —*Matisse on Matisse (1908)*

Drawing with Color The Fauves were not particularly interested in depicting reality. They painted for the sheer joy of painting—as a way of expressing themselves. Many viewers at that time called their work violent. But a close look reveals that the Fauves actually demonstrated much skill and discipline in their work.

Matisse's painting *Joy of Life* is one example. It shows a group of nude figures dancing in a forest clearing. In a way, the scene is similar in setting and composition to those painted by Classical artists of the past. The broad areas of color are carefully balanced. But Matisse's lines are almost like shorthand. Although they are simple and spare, they clearly describe the trees and people. It is obvious from the shapes and postures of the dancing figures that Matisse understood human anatomy.

Matisse's *Harmony in Red* shows his skill with decoration. In the painting, a red tablecloth exactly matches the room's red wallpaper. Matisse used repeating shapes, colors, and decorative elements to achieve his "harmony." Everything in the painting is part of a colorful pattern.

In 1943, Matisse moved to Vence in southern France. In gratitude to the Dominican sisters who nursed him through a serious illness, he designed and financed this chapel for them.

After Fauvism

What united the Fauves most was a sense of experimentation with color, form, line, and even brush strokes. After just a few years, their experimentation took each of them in a different direction. Dufy became more traditional. Braque tried the sharp angles of Cubism. Rouault explored the new personal and emotional styles of Expressionism. The group disbanded.

Following the breakup of the Fauves, Matisse continued to explore artistic styles. He tried the geometric approach of the Cubists. He did sculpture, book illustration, and architectural decoration. When his health began to fail in the 1940s, he worked in *découpées,* which are colorful paper cutouts on white backgrounds. He was able to make these cutouts while lying in bed.

One of Matisse's last projects was decorating the chapel at a convent of Dominican nuns in the French town of Vence. He did the work out of gratitude to one of the sisters. She had nursed him through his recovery from surgery several years earlier.

Henri Matisse died in 1954 at the age of 85. Half a century earlier, he had shocked the art world. But by the end of his life, he had inspired two generations of artists. In doing so, he had become one of the most influential artists of the 20th century.

Pablo Picasso

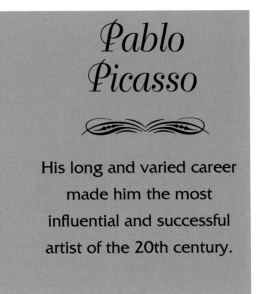

His long and varied career made him the most influential and successful artist of the 20th century.

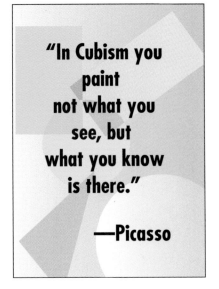

"In Cubism you paint not what you see, but what you know is there."

—Picasso

In the early 1900s, Picasso experimented with a new style. Critics, who saw only sharp edges and angles, called the new style Cubism.

Geometric Art

Picasso had studied the work of French painter Paul Cézanne. Cézanne believed that all natural objects were based on three geometric shapes: the cone, the sphere, and the cylinder. Picasso admired Cézanne's work. He also admired the primitive qualities of African and Oceanic sculpture. He brought elements of both together in a new style that became known as *Cubism*.

Picasso's first Cubist painting was *Les Demoiselles d'Avignon* (The Young Ladies of Avignon). This painting of five women was so unusual that it even shocked Henri Matisse, who was himself an innovative artist. In Picasso's painting, sharp angles distort the shape of the women's bodies. The limbs are out of proportion. The mask-like features seem to be out of place. By his use of these nontraditional elements, Picasso challenged the Classical ideals of beauty. One critic said that the painting "resembles a field of broken glass." It was as if Picasso had taken apart all the pieces and reassembled them in a different order.

Like Father, Like Son

Born in Málaga, Spain, in 1881, Pablo Ruiz y Picasso showed enormous talent, even as a young child. His father, a painter and professor of art, recognized and encouraged young Pablo's interest in art. Pablo Picasso studied at the finest art schools in Barcelona and Madrid. He quickly mastered the traditional art training. His early drawings demonstrate outstanding skill. According to one story, Picasso's father was so impressed with his son's work that he gave his own brushes and palette to the boy.

Blue Period Pablo Picasso first visited Paris in 1900, at the age of 19. He did not speak French, and he knew very few people there. His paintings during this time reflect his feelings of loneliness and despair. *The Old Guitarist* is a typical painting from his so-called *Blue Period.* His subjects were sad, downtrodden people, and he painted them in various shades of blue.

By 1904, Picasso was settled in Paris and had a major exhibit in the city. He had a wide circle of friends that included many young artists and writers. In this happier time, Picasso painted the clowns and jugglers of his *Rose Period.* Picasso did not remain in the Rose Period for long. By 1907, he had moved on to another style.

Pablo Picasso had a long and productive career. He experimented with a variety of styles, materials, and art forms.

Shape of Things to Come Around the same time that Picasso was painting *Les Demoiselles,* Georges Braque (formerly one of the Fauves) was developing a similar Cubist style. Braque worked with Picasso for a time, and it is difficult to tell some of their work apart.

Whether they painted still lifes or portraits, the Cubists broke down their three-dimensional subjects into simple shapes, then put them together again. During the most extreme phase of Cubism (called *Analytic Cubism*),

In *Three Musicians* (1921), Pablo Picasso combined the sharp angles of Cubism and the vivid colors of Fauvism. The result is a joyous painting, nearly seven feet high.

the paintings resembled what a viewer might see if he or she looked at the object through a prism.

By 1912, Picasso and Braque were attaching real objects—such as pieces of chair caning or newspaper clippings—to their canvases. This technique became known as *Collage* Cubism, from the French word for "pasteup." Eventually, Picasso stopped using objects and began to paint as if he were gluing brightly colored shapes to his canvas. *Three Musicians* is an example of the later Cubism— forms reduced to simple, flat geometric shapes and vibrant color.

Picasso extended Cubism to his sculpture. His sculpture called *Head of a Woman* shows the same sharp angles as appear in his paintings and the same "found" objects (springs and colanders) as in his collages.

Torn by War For most of his life, Picasso was more interested in art than in politics. During the Spanish Civil War, however, Picasso became involved on the side of the Loyalists (defenders of the republic), who were fighting against Fascist leader Francisco Franco. In 1937, Franco had allowed the Nazi air force to bomb the militarily insignificant Spanish village of Guernica. The raid, which killed many civilians, was a practice run for the bombings that became common during World War II.

After the air raid, Picasso painted a huge canvas, which he called *Guernica*. More than 11 feet tall and 25 feet wide, the painting depicts the horrors of war. The powerfully emotional scene is painted entirely in black, white, and gray. The figures include a mother sobbing over a dying child, a horse howling in agony, and a terrified woman looking through a window. Like Goya before him, Pablo Picasso was appalled at man's inhumanity to man.

Evolution Continues

Picasso's work throughout World War II was somber. When the Nazi concentration camps were discovered at the end of the war, Picasso painted *The Charnel House*. (A charnel house is a place where bones and bodies are deposited.) Like *Guernica, The Charnel House* was the artist's reaction to the atrocities of war.

After the war, Picasso moved to the French Riviera, in southern France. There he helped revive the local pottery industry. If the great Picasso was making pottery, people thought, it must be art. Picasso's venture into printmaking revived that art form as well.

No single form of artistic expression satisfied Pablo Picasso for long. He continued to change styles, and he never stopped experimenting. He was remarkably productive well into his old age. During seven months of 1968, Picasso, then 87, produced a series of nearly 350 prints. Two years later, he held his last major exhibition. He died in 1973. His career had spanned nearly a century and had changed modern art forever.

Picasso produced several humorous statues, such as this *She-Goat,* which was sculpted in 1950.

Diego Rivera

The works
of this leading
Mexican muralist
helped introduce
European Modernism
to the Americas.

As a young man, Rivera lived and worked among a group of politically conscious artists and writers. Political themes are an important part of his work. Rivera was influenced by the frescoes of the Italian masters Giotto, da Vinci, and Michelangelo and by the folk art of Mexico.

Early Political Awareness

Democratic Ideals Twin boys were born to the Rivera family in Guanajuato, Mexico, in 1886. One of the boys, José Carlos, died before he was two. The other, Diego, began to draw at age three. When Diego Rivera grew up, he would become the leader of the mural-painting movement that flourished in his country after the Revolution of 1910.

Rivera's father was a teacher and political activist who called for changes in the government and the social structure. He expressed his views in the newspaper *El Democrata* (The Democrat). His views were revolutionary and unpopular with the people of Guanajuato. When Diego was six, the Rivera family moved to Mexico City.

Young Rebel At the age of ten, Diego Rivera received a government scholarship that enabled him to study art at the Academy of San Carlos. When he was 16, he was expelled from the academy for participating in a student strike. Although he was later reinstated, he never returned to the school.

Larger Than Life

Rivera worked on his own for the next five years. In 1907, he won a scholarship to study in Europe. His first stop was Spain. From there, he traveled throughout Europe. While living in Europe, mostly in Paris, he became friends with some of the leading modern artists—Georges Braque, Pablo Picasso, and the Swiss painter Paul Klee.

On the eve of the Mexican Revolution in 1910, Rivera made a brief trip to Mexico for an exhibition of his work. He returned to France a few weeks after the Mexican dictator, Porfirio Díaz, resigned. For the next ten years, he lived and worked among the politically conscious artists and writers in Paris. He also became acquainted with a group of Russian exiles living there and adopted many of their Communist ideas.

During this time, civil war erupted in Mexico. Rivera sympathized with the peasants and the working class. Although they were a majority, these people had little money or land, and virtually no political power. Rivera wanted to find a way to convey his sympathies and revolutionary ideals through his art. After a year in Italy, where he studied Renaissance frescoes, Rivera returned to Mexico City.

Art and Politics In the early 1900s, many Mexicans could not read. Much of their education came from the religious murals in the churches they attended. The new political leaders thought that large public artworks would be the best way to promote their ideas for reform.

The Ministry of Education commissioned Rivera to paint a series of murals for the *Preparatoria* (National Preparatory School). Rivera traveled to Mexico's Yucatán Peninsula to

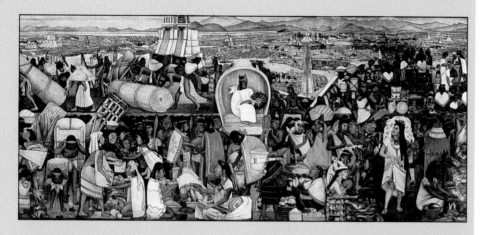

Rivera painted many large murals dealing with the lives, history, and social problems of the Mexican people. He painted *The Marketsquare of Tlatelolco* for the National Museum in Mexico City.

study the ancient art in the abandoned cities of Chichén Itzá and Uxmal. The murals that Rivera painted for the school combined Aztec and Mayan elements with the Expressionism and Cubism that he had studied in Europe.

In 1922, Diego Rivera joined the Communist Party—a move that would later cause him difficulty in his professional life. Rivera's murals—124 frescoes in all—showed farmers and working people, soldiers and revolutionary heroes. A group of students, who opposed the revolutionary government, protested Rivera's Preparatoria murals. The protest was so threatening to the artist that he kept a pistol in his belt as he continued to work on the frescoes.

North of the Border Rivera's success in Mexico earned him acclaim in the United States as well. He received several important commissions—*Allegory of California* for the San Francisco Stock Exchange and *The Making of a Fresco* for the California School of Fine Arts. In 1931, his show at the Museum of Modern Art in New York City broke all attendance records and made him an instant celebrity.

Rivera completed a series of murals for the Detroit Institute of Art. One, part of a 27-panel fresco called *Detroit Industry,* shows the production of Ford Motor Company's new V-8 engine. In 1933, when the murals were dedicated, they were seen by more than 86,000 visitors.

With the Detroit project completed, Rivera went to New York to paint a mural in the new RCA Building at Rockefeller Center. It soon became known that the mural showed Vladimir Lenin, head of the Communist Party, and his supporters. Nelson Rockefeller, whose family owned the center, wanted the mural changed. Rivera said that he would rather see the mural destroyed, although he did offer to replace Lenin with Abraham Lincoln. The management at RCA fired Rivera and later destroyed the mural.

The success of Rivera and other Mexican muralists during the 1920s encouraged the idea of a popular public art in the United States. It is ironic that these works that glorified revolution inspired the establishment of the Federal Arts Project in the United States. This project helped many unemployed American artists survive the Great Depression of the 1930s.

Too Radical

Tarnished Reputation Despite the influence that Diego Rivera's work had in the United States, he did not receive many more commissions in the United States or in Mexico. His radical politics were unpopular in both countries. Even the Communist Party leaders thought that he was too headstrong and expelled him from the party. They were angry about an unflattering portrait he had painted of Soviet dictator Joseph Stalin.

The People's Painter In 1957, Rivera died of a heart attack. Throughout his career, he had collected pre-Columbian (made before the arrival of Columbus) Mexican art. He left his collection to the people of Mexico.

MAKING A FRESCO

1. The artist makes a cartoon (a sketch the exact size of the proposed picture) on paper of medium thickness.

2. Fresh plaster is laid onto the surface that is to be painted. Only a small area is covered at a time—usually the amount of space the artist can paint in a sitting. The plaster cannot be painted on after it has dried.

3. The artist places a section of the cartoon on the wet plaster and carves the design onto the plaster with a sharp tool.

4. The artist brushes on the watercolors. The drying paint unites chemically with the lime in the plaster, binding the paint to the wall.

5. Any unpainted plaster must be cut away.

Fresco is the Italian word for fresh and is used to describe painting on freshly laid wet plaster. The steps in producing a fresco are listed here.

Ludwig Mies van der Rohe

As one of the founders of the International Style, he greatly influenced modern architecture.

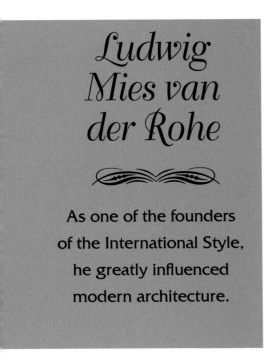

In the 20th century, styles in architecture went from highly decorated buildings, such as the Chrysler Building in New York City, to unadorned straight lines.

The Bauhaus

Slow to Change Architectural styles change more slowly than other forms of art. Like large, monumental sculptures, buildings are meant to be public structures. They also are expensive to design and construct. As a result, architecture tends to be conservative, with few extreme changes. The most original designs rarely leave the architect's drawing board. Unlike painters, architects have little opportunity to experiment.

A notable exception occurred in Germany in the 1920s following the German defeat in World War I and the overthrow of the German emperor. The new architectural style that was developed there became the major force in modern architecture.

Clean Lines The *Bauhaus,* which means "building house," was founded in 1919 as a state school of the arts. Walter Gropius, its founder and director, encouraged students to express modern ideas in their work. He believed that buildings should be simple and functional. He promoted the use of basic materials and clean lines with little decoration. Students at the Bauhaus studied mechanical crafts, aesthetics (concepts of beauty), materials, sociology, and accounting. Gropius considered all these subjects necessary for combining architecture with modern technology. The designs that were developed here were part of what came to be known as the International Style.

The New Idealists

German architect Mies van der Rohe taught at the Bauhaus. His designs for glass skyscrapers earned him the reputation as a leading *avant-garde* architect. *Avant-garde* is a French term that refers to those who develop and use new techniques in their fields, especially in the arts. In 1927, a group of German industrialists and artists asked Mies to put together a major architectural exhibition in Stuttgart. They also asked Mies to design a housing project for the exhibition.

The Stuttgart show was an enormous success. As a result, Mies received a commission to design the German Pavilion for the 1929 International Exhibition in Spain. The pavilion sat on a marble base as if it were a sculpture. The building's walls were made of glass and polished marble, and the roof sat on chrome-steel columns. The building was remarkable for its simplicity. Mies's motto was "Less is more." He believed, as the ancient Greeks had, that simplicity was essential to good design. The pavilion was considered by many to be one of the best examples of 20th-century architecture.

Glass Houses Mies van der Rohe succeeded Gropius as director of the Bauhaus in 1930. That year, he also designed the Tugendhat House in Czechoslovakia. The house featured walls of glass that blurred the boundary between indoors and outdoors. Mies designed the interior of the house with columns instead of walls for support. In this way, one room flowed into the next. The furniture that he designed for the house had the same spare look and clean lines as the house itself.

The effect of the building was dramatically different from anything seen before. Some people objected.

The glass walls made them feel exposed. The open spaces made them uncomfortable. But the overall response to the Tugendhat House was favorable. The public liked the clean, airy look.

Coming to America The architects of the International Style were generally as forward-looking in their politics as they were in their art. The Nazis found the Bauhaus ideas too radical and "un-German." In 1933, Nazi leader Adolf Hitler closed the school.

Mies came to the United States and became the director of the Armour Institute in Chicago (now the Illinois Institute of Technology). One of his projects there was to design Crown Hall. The building illustrates his belief that each part of the structure should be designed in accordance with its function, and that the building itself should harmonize with its surroundings.

In the 1950s, Mies designed an apartment complex along Chicago's Lake Shore Drive. These famous high-rise buildings stand like giant slabs of glass and black steel. The extremely sleek and simple design is radically different from the ornately decorated apartment buildings constructed in the first half of the century.

Another well-known Mies work is the Seagram Building in New York City. For this spectacular 38-story office building, Mies omitted the traditional spire that topped most skyscrapers. He believed that materials, not ornaments, should provide decoration. For the exterior of the building, he used bronze-tinted glass walls instead of windows and insisted on bronze for the interior walls. Although bronze was expensive, it achieved the impressive and luxurious effect he wanted.

The Seagram Building, which Mies van der Rohe designed in the 1950s, lacked the traditional ornamentation of other New York skyscrapers.

Crystal Cities

Urban architects were copying the Seagram Building even before it was completed. During the construction boom of the 1950s and 1960s, tall glass buildings were reshaping the skylines of U.S. cities.

The architects of the International Style had a lasting effect. Most of today's sleek office towers owe their appearance to the artistic ideals of Mies van der Rohe and his contemporaries.

BUILDINGS DESIGNED BY LUDWIG MIES VAN DER ROHE		
Date	**Building**	**Location**
1907	Riehl House	Berlin-Neubabelsberg, Germany
1926–27	Municipal Housing Development	Berlin
1929	German Pavilion, International Exhibition	Barcelona, Spain
1939–58	Alumni Memorial Hall, Library and Administration Building, Chemistry Building, and others at the Illinois Institute of Technology	Chicago
1948–51	Lake Shore Drive Apartments	Chicago
1954–58	Seagram Building, Park Avenue	New York City
1957–61	Bacardi Office Building	Mexico City
1958	Brown Pavilion, Museum of Fine Arts	Houston
1959–64	Chicago Federal Center	Chicago
1962–68	New National Gallery	West Berlin
1963	Lafayette Towers, Lafayette Park	Detroit
1967	Mansion House Square Project	London

This is a partial listing of the more than 150 buildings designed by Mies van der Rohe. His work includes office towers, apartment houses, university buildings, courthouses, and a power station.

Georgia O'Keeffe

Struggling to achieve recognition in a male-dominated field, O'Keeffe created her own highly individual style of painting.

Child of the Plains

Born in 1887, Georgia Totto O'Keeffe grew up on a farm outside Sun Prairie, Wisconsin. As a child, she spent a great deal of time outdoors, observing the changing seasons and growth cycles of the trees and flowers around her. Nature eventually would become a major inspiration for her work.

O'Keeffe and her sisters were given lessons in painting and drawing. Before she had even reached her teens, Georgia O'Keeffe knew that she wanted to become an artist. She studied at the Art Institute of Chicago and at the Art Students League in New York City. She did well and even won a scholarship for her work. But she felt that her work reflected what her teachers wanted—not what she herself wanted to paint.

Family financial problems forced O'Keeffe to leave school and take an advertising job drawing lace. After a serious case of measles affected her eyesight, O'Keeffe left the job. From 1911 to 1918, she taught art in various schools in Texas, Virginia, and South Carolina.

Her Talent Blossoms

During this time, O'Keeffe renewed her interest in painting. She took classes and experimented with different styles, trying to find the one that expressed the way she felt.

In 1915, she decided to forget everything she had been taught in art school and go back to the basics. She spent her days teaching. At night, she experimented with black-and-white

charcoal drawings of abstract shapes. These drawings, she felt, expressed her feelings. O'Keeffe was pleased with her drawings, but she wanted a second opinion. She sent a batch of her drawings to Anita Pollitzer, a friend who lived in New York City.

Pollitzer sent O'Keeffe's drawings to Alfred Stieglitz, a prominent photographer and art dealer. He was so enthusiastic about O'Keeffe's work, he immediately displayed the drawings in his gallery—without the artist's permission. O'Keeffe soon learned about the exhibit and demanded that Stieglitz remove her work. He persuaded her to keep the drawings in the show.

The following year, Georgia O'Keeffe painted a series of watercolors in vivid colors. Stieglitz exhibited this work in a one-woman show in the spring of 1917. He also offered to support O'Keeffe for a year so that she

The mountains of New Mexico, seen from the window of her studio, provided O'Keeffe with a rich source of material for her work.

34

◀ Fascinated by the variety of shapes and colors of flowers, Georgia O'Keeffe painted hundreds of close-up views. This painting is called *Yellow Hickory Leaves with Daisy* (1928).

could concentrate her energy on her painting. He also began photographing her. Eventually, Stieglitz would take more than 500 photographs of O'Keeffe. The couple were married in 1923, and Stieglitz continued to promote her work.

Shapes and Colors Influenced by her husband's work, O'Keeffe used many photographic techniques in her oil paintings. For example, she painted extreme close-ups of individual flowers, but she simplified what she saw. She was fascinated by the shapes and colors of flowers, and she painted many of them. Hers are abstract and colorful. In the painting called *Yellow Hickory Leaves with Daisy*, the yellow leaves fill the canvas from top to bottom. The lines are soft, but the image is strong and powerful.

O'Keeffe also painted a series of urban skylines during the time that she and Stieglitz lived in New York City. She followed the geometric style that was popular at the time. Sometimes she painted recognizable objects, and sometimes not. Although her paintings were highly praised and sold for high prices, O'Keeffe felt that something was missing in her art.

The Great Southwest On a trip to New Mexico in 1929, O'Keeffe found what was missing. In the Southwest, she fell in love again with the vast open spaces, reminiscent of her childhood in the Midwest. The desert became her major source of inspiration. From then on, she spent several months of every year in the Southwest, painting the land and the objects she found there.

O'Keeffe painted many canvases that combine the landscape and animal bones. In one such painting, *From the Faraway Nearby,* a large pair of elk antlers seems to advance toward the viewer while snowcapped mountains stand in the far distance.

Later Years

After Stieglitz died in 1946, O'Keeffe moved permanently to New Mexico. She established memorials to her late husband and donated his extensive art collection to several museums. For the next dozen or so years, she traveled throughout the world, always returning to her beloved home in Abiquiu. She painted until the 1970s, when her eyesight failed. She remained in New Mexico until her death in 1986.

During her long career, Georgia O'Keeffe received numerous honors. She was elected to the American Academy of Arts and Letters in 1963 and to the American Academy of Arts and Sciences in 1966. Exhibitions of her work have been in major U.S. museums, including the Whitney Museum of American Art in New York City, the Art Institute of Chicago, and the National Gallery of Art in Washington, D.C.

Georgia O'Keeffe's simple, bold landscapes and still lifes are among the most original American paintings of the 20th century. In her paintings, O'Keeffe provided viewers with her special vision of America—a land that is vast and unspoiled. O'Keeffe's productive career did much to pave the way for women artists in a male-dominated field.

WOMEN ARTISTS

Artist	Country	Work	Date
Lavinia Fontana	Italy	*Portrait of a Noblewoman*	1580
Judith Leyster	Netherlands	*The Merry Drinker*	1629
Rachel Ruysch	Netherlands	*Flower Still Life*	after 1700
Rosalba Carriera	Italy	*Woman at Her Dressing Table*	c. 1730
Élisabeth Vigée-Lebrun	France	*Marie Antoinette and Her Children*	1787
Sarah Miriam Peale	United States	*A Slice of Watermelon*	1825
Rosa Bonheur	France	*The Horse Fair*	1855
Berthe Morisot	France	*The Sisters*	1869
Mary Cassatt	United States	*Peasant Mother and Child*	1894
Käthe Kollwitz	Germany	*Whetting the Scythe*	1905
Frida Kahlo	Mexico	*Self-Portrait with Cropped Hair*	1940

Although there have been women artists throughout history, only a few have gained recognition in this male-dominated field.

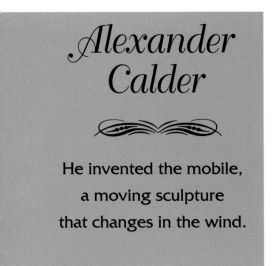

Alexander Calder

He invented the mobile,
a moving sculpture
that changes in the wind.

In his studio in Roxbury, Connecticut, Calder created his delicate and playful mobiles and his monumental stabiles.

Three Generations

At the turn of the 20th century, a family of sculptors thrived in Philadelphia. Alexander Milne Calder had produced the statue of William Penn and the four bronze eagles atop Philadelphia's City Hall. His son, Alexander Stirling Calder, had sculpted the graceful statues for the fountain in Logan Square, a few blocks away. But it was Alexander Calder of the next generation who invented a whole new kind of sculpture by adding motion to sculpted works. One of his unique moving sculptures, called *mobiles,* hangs inside the entrance to the Philadelphia Museum of Art, near Logan Square. A visitor to the museum can stand in the doorway and see the evolution of modern sculpture through the work of three generations of Calders.

Aimless Engineer Alexander Calder attended college because it was expected of him. He decided to study mechanical engineering. Following his graduation in 1919, he worked at various jobs, including insurance investigator, lumberjack, and fireman on board a ship. He drifted from one unsatisfying job to the next, until a family friend gave him some advice. The friend, who worked for a Canadian engineering firm, told young Calder that he had always regretted not becoming an architect. "He advised me to do what I really wanted to do . . . ," Calder later recalled in his memoirs. "So, I decided to become a painter."

A Working Artist Calder spent two years at the Art Students League in New York City. To earn money during this time, he made line drawings for the *National Police Gazette.* After leaving art school, he produced paintings for the advertising brochures of a steamship cruise line. This work took him across the ocean. In 1926, he set up a studio in Paris. There he sculpted animals from wood and wire. In some of his works, he imitated the abstract and whimsical shapes of Piet Mondrian and Joan Miró, both well-known painters of the time.

The piece that brought Calder the most attention at this point in his career was *The Circus,* which he completed in 1927. It consisted of a miniature circus tent with wood and wire marionettes that moved. To earn rent money, Calder exhibited his elaborate "toy." Over the next few years, Calder had many requests to present *The Circus* at private parties and in his studio.

Calder liked the idea that his creations moved. He continued to experiment with some mechanical sculptures, using pulleys and small motors to move the parts. Although Calder liked the concept of movement, he soon became bored with the predictable motion of the pulley- and motor-driven pieces. He was ready for something new.

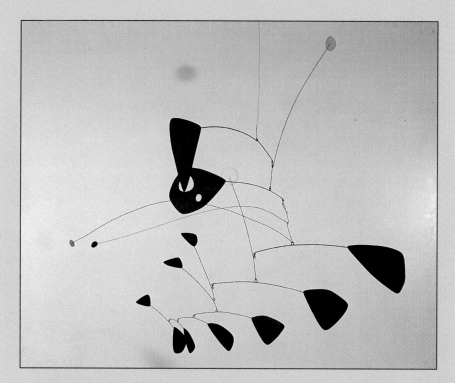

Calder's work is exhibited throughout the world. This mobile, called *Antennae with Red and Blue Dots*, is in the Tate Gallery in London. Like many of his other mobiles, it is made of rods, wires, and metal forms so carefully balanced that even the slightest air current moves its parts in a planned pattern.

Another Dimension

Blowing in the Wind In the early 1930s, Calder found the answer to his quest for spontaneous movement—it was wind. At first, he cut abstract shapes from sheets of aluminum, steel, and brass. Then he wired them together and hung them. With his knowledge of engineering, Calder could balance the pieces perfectly, so that they moved smoothly and rhythmically in the slightest breeze. The composition of the work—the relationship of the individual pieces to one another—changed constantly.

Abstract painter Marcel Duchamp called Calder's sculptures *mobiles,* from the French word for "movable." Duchamp also organized the first exhibition of Calder's mobiles in Paris in 1932. That same year, the mobiles were shown in the United States.

Natural Reactions Although Calder's sculptures look mechanical, they are "natural." *Lobster Trap and Fish Tail* imitates the soothing motion of the sea. *The Ghost* twists and turns like an airy spirit. How his works move depends on the air currents in the environment in which they are displayed.

Calder's *Spiral,* shown here at UNESCO headquarters in Paris, combines moving and stationary elements.

Stop Action

Calder's mobiles were immediately popular, and he received commissions throughout the world. He created all kinds and all sizes, including some that were used in stage sets that he designed for dancer Martha Graham.

During World War II, when metal was scarce, Calder began making stationary sculptures, mostly out of wood. These works are called *stabiles.* One of his later and most impressive stabiles is the 95-foot-high stainless steel *Man,* which he made for the Montreal World's Fair in 1967. His colossal abstract stabiles stand in open spaces in cities throughout the world. *The Whirling Ear* in Brussels was a gift from the United States to the people of that Belgian city. Another Calder work, *The Spiral*—which combines moving and stationary elements—adorns the UNESCO Headquarters in Paris.

In his long and successful career, Calder produced numerous works known for their wit and good humor. In 1964, the Guggenheim Museum in New York held a major retrospective of his work—an exhibit of 361 Calder works. *The Circus,* which he refined and added to over the years, is often exhibited at the Whitney Museum of American Art in New York.

Alexander Calder, who died in 1976, was perhaps the most original sculptor of the 20th century. He certainly had the most distinctive style. He produced a body of work that continues to delight viewers. Every baby who is entertained by a mobile over his or her crib owes thanks to this innovative artist.

Henry Spencer Moore

His monumental
free-form sculptures
bring to mind primitive
gods and goddesses.

Schoolboy to Sculptor

Henry Moore's first carving still hangs in the school he attended in Yorkshire, England. The wooden plaque he carved to honor the Castleford Secondary School students who fought in World War I is rather ordinary. It offers no hints about the unique stone and brass monuments for which this sculptor eventually would become famous.

Moore was born in 1898, the son of a coal miner. As a child, he wanted to become a sculptor—like the great Michelangelo. At 17, Moore joined the army, serving as the youngest member of his regiment in World War I. After the war ended, he received an army scholarship to attend the Leeds School of Art. He showed exceptional talent and earned a second scholarship—this time to the Royal College of Art in London. His studies included drawing, painting, and modeling in clay.

Modern Primitive

Moore often visited the museums in London. But two of these places— the British Museum's Ethnographic Gallery and the Museum of Natural History—had a particular influence on his work. The Ethnographic Gallery is dedicated to the study of different cultures. Moore was inspired by the primitive sculptures from Egypt, Mexico, Peru, China, and the South Pacific islands that he saw in the gallery. He also was fascinated by the shapes of skeletons, stones, and other objects on display in the Museum of Natural History. He himself was a collector of stones and other natural items.

Simplicity in Stone Inspired by his museum visits, Moore began to carve large, abstract figures from natural materials. His first one-man show in 1926 led to a major commission—a work for the headquarters of the London Underground, the city's subway system. Called *North Wind,* this simple, massive figure is carved from stone and is typical of Moore's works. He carved stone and other materials in such a way that his work looks like the result of natural forces—wind and water—over time.

Moore carved many works of women reclining, or lying down. One of these, called *Recumbent Figure,* resembled the primitive statues Moore had seen at the Ethnographic Gallery.

Many of Moore's sculptures have large holes in them. Although holes were not an original idea, Moore was the first sculptor to make the hole an important part of the work. He believed that the hole gave the sculpture depth and enabled the viewer to see the back while looking at the front.

Once, when commissioned to sculpt a piece for a town square, Moore was asked "not to leave any holes where boys could trap their heads." This sculpture, called *Oval with Points,* is on the campus of Princeton University in New Jersey.

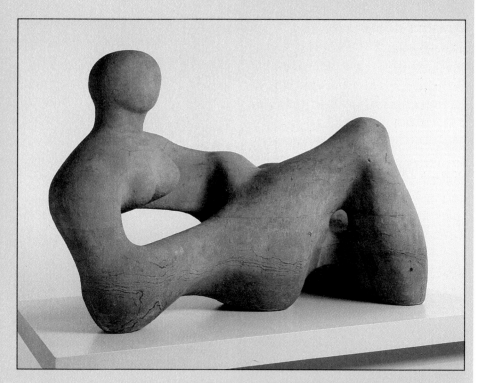

Although the human figure is clearly recognizable in *Reclining Figure*, it is reduced to an abstract form that seems to be a part of the environment.

New Directions

In the decade following the war, Moore's sculpture changed in an important way. As a younger man, he had preferred carving natural materials, such as wood and stone. As he grew older, however, he modeled most of his works in clay. Then he cast them in bronze.

One important work from the postwar period is the bronze *King and Queen,* which Moore finished in 1953. The bodies of the two figures are wide curved sheets of bronze that sit on a low bench. Their heads are imaginative shapes that combine face and crown. A single hole represents the king's two eyes.

Working in clay and bronze had some advantages for Moore. He could make more than one piece from the cast. He could make larger pieces, such as the massive *Reclining Figure* that he sculpted for Lincoln Center in New York City in 1965. And, after Moore completed the clay model, his assistants could cast the bronze for him. Using clay enabled him to work faster. He had many creative ideas that he wanted to express through his art. Moore continued to work almost until his death in 1986 at the age of 88.

Moore liked the holes for another reason. They were mysterious, he said, like caves. This made his figures seem more like earth goddesses. The plain curved pieces could be seen as reclining women or as rolling hills with caves.

Dark Tunnels Caves and tunnels also appeared in Moore's drawings. When World War II broke out, Moore and his family were living outside London. On a trip to the city, he learned that Londoners were sleeping in the subway stations. These underground shelters protected them from German bombs. Moore visited the subway shelters and made a series of drawings of the frightened people huddled in the tunnels. The shapes of the people in these pictures were very much like the shapes of his sculptures. They had a mythic, almost religious, quality that touched the viewer's emotions.

Moore's World War II drawings were immediately popular and highly praised. The War Artists Advisory Committee commissioned several works. The committee also sent Moore to his native Yorkshire to draw coal miners there. This art was done in recognition of the miners' war work—supplying badly needed fuel.

In 1943, Moore returned to sculpture. In that year, the Church of Saint Matthew's in Northampton commissioned him to do a madonna and child. Three years later, his own daughter was born. Her birth may have been the inspiration for him to do several variations on the madonna-and-child theme.

Early in his career, Moore was a carver. Later, he preferred to model his works in clay and then to cast them in bronze.

Ansel Adams

The beauty
of his photographs
helped preserve
much of America's
wilderness.

A Boy's Life

Ansel Adams was born in San Francisco in 1902. From his childhood home on the sand dunes outside the city, Adams could see both mountains and ocean. It is, therefore, no surprise that nature would become his favorite photographic subject.

Adams was restless in school, so his father had him tutored at home. The elder Adams took an active role in his son's education, exposing him to the writings of American essayist Ralph Waldo Emerson. Emerson encouraged his readers to act on their beliefs. Young Adams took this advice to heart and was an environmental activist throughout his life.

Adams learned much about the outdoors from his father. He also was greatly influenced by a book about the western wilderness called *In the Heart of the Sierras,* which he read during his early teen years. But it was a family vacation to Yosemite National Park when he was 16 that completely changed the course of his life.

Music and Vision

Adams had his first camera—a Kodak Box Brownie—with him on that trip. He was thrilled by the beauty he saw. The photographs he took reflected his feelings for Yosemite.

Following the family's vacation, Adams joined the Sierra Club, an organization that promotes conservation of the wilderness. For several years, Adams divided his time between playing the piano and working for the club. He led hikes in the Sierra Nevada mountains, photographed the treks, and wrote about them for the *Sierra Club Bulletin.*

Adams studied piano for many years, and for a time he considered a career in music. His music studies taught him about the nature of perfection and the importance of practice for mastering a skill.

Throughout his career, Adams shot mostly in black and white, carefully choosing film, lenses, and filters to obtain the picture he wanted. He studied the effect of changing light on his subject, taking some of his best photographs in the dramatic light of early morning or early evening. He captured the emotional experience of being the "first" to see the majesty of the wilderness. The well-known

> "I believe photography has both a challenge and an obligation: to help us see more clearly and more deeply, and to reveal to others the grandeurs and the potentials of the one and only world which we inhabit."
>
> —Ansel Adams, 1/22/69

Adams's philosophy, as expressed here, explains his lifelong work as an environmentalist.

photograph *Monolith, the Face of Half Dome* (a mountain in Yosemite) is an outstanding example of the majesty he sought to depict.

Sharper Focus In 1929, Adams met photographer Paul Strand. Through his friendship with Strand, Adams decided to concentrate his efforts on photography and within a few years, Adams had his first show. In 1933, he opened a gallery in San Francisco.

Adams and several other San Francisco Bay area photographers were dissatisfied with the photography of the time—impressionistic pictures shot in soft focus. They formed

Adams set out to develop a photographic style that was completely his own. He took great care in choosing lenses, lighting, and angles that would enhance his vision.

Group f/64, named for the camera setting that gave the sharpest focus. The group's style, which emphasized tones and sharp detail, was to have a major influence on the history of photography.

Adams taught photographic technique and wrote several books on the subject. He developed a system that divides the tonal scale for black and white photos into 11 zones—from zone 0 (black) to zone 10 (white). This system enabled photographers to achieve the desired effects of contrast in their prints.

A Picture's Worth Adams's images of Yosemite, Northern California, Alaska, and Colorado were so powerful that in 1936 the Sierra Club sent him to Washington, D.C. The club's officials hoped that Adams and his photographs would help persuade Congress to establish a national park—Kings Canyon—in the southern Sierras. Secretary of the Interior Harold Ickes was so impressed with Adams's work that he asked the photographer to do a photomural for the Department of the Interior building in the nation's capital. And Kings Canyon National Park was opened in 1940.

Adams took some of his best-known photographs during World War II. He wanted to show Americans what they were fighting to preserve. His pictures of Mount Williamson, the Grand Tetons, and the Snake River immortalized the American landscape. One image from this time, called *Moonrise, Hernandez, New Mexico,* shows the moon rising against a black sky. This is perhaps the most famous photograph in the world.

Long after the war ended, Adams continued to encourage Americans to appreciate their wildlands. In 1960, the Sierra Club published his photographs in a book called *This Is the American Earth.* The book helped win support for the growing environmental movement.

Letter Campaign Working with environmentalists, Adams wrote hundreds of letters to government officials. He fought to prevent the construction of a dam across the Grand Canyon, a campaign that was won. Later, he joined the Wilderness Society in its efforts to remove James Watt from office. Watt was a controversial secretary of the interior who favored development over preservation of the nation's wilderness areas.

President Carter presented the Medal of Freedom to Ansel Adams for his artistic and environmental work.

Man and Mountain

Adams was rewarded for his artistic and his environmental work. In 1980, President Jimmy Carter awarded Adams the Presidential Medal of Freedom. That same year, the Wilderness Society established the Ansel Adams Award for lifetime service to conservation.

During Adams's lifetime, millions of acres of open land in the United States were preserved. Much of that preservation was due—directly or indirectly—to his efforts.

Ansel Adams died in 1984 at the age of 82. That year, Congress established the 220,000-acre Ansel Adams Wilderness in the Sierras. In his beloved Yosemite, which he visited every year of his life, a peak was named for him—Mount Ansel Adams.

The principal subject matter of Adams's photographs was always the unspoiled natural world. He shot this view of the Canyon de Chelly in Arizona from a nearby mountain.

Salvador Dali

This 20th-century Spanish painter put his dreams on canvas.

The Mind's Eye

Throughout cultural history, attitudes have swung back and forth between reason and emotion. The restraint of the Renaissance was followed by the excesses of the Baroque period. Later, the Romantics rebelled against the Classical tradition. In the early 20th century, another trend entered the picture.

A new field of medicine, called psychiatry, was trying to understand emotions in a logical way. One of the first and most famous psychiatrists was the Austrian Sigmund Freud. Dr. Freud emphasized the importance of the subconscious—that part of the mind that is below the surface of our conscious thoughts and actions. He believed that fantasies and dreams were the keys to unlocking the secrets of the subconscious.

More Real Than Reality

Among those who read and supported Freud's theories was a group of artists and writers who wanted to do more than just copy reality. Their work came to be known as *Surrealism,* meaning "super realism." French poet André Breton founded the Surrealist movement in Paris in 1924. He believed that rational thought interfered with creativity. In other words, real creativity came from the subconscious.

The Surrealists, as the group came to be called, were not the first painters to put their fantasies on canvas. Francisco Goya and 20th-century painters Marc Chagall and Giorgio de Chirico had created works from their imaginations. But one painter, Salvador Dali, went a step further.

In Touch with Dreams

Salvador Dali was born in Figueras, Spain, in 1904. Like many other artists, he showed his talent early. Dali had his first show when he was 14. Three years later, he enrolled at the Academy of Fine Arts in Madrid.

Dali's artistic skills were highly developed already. His teachers at the academy had little to teach him—and he let them know it! At the school, Dali became friends with others who shared his interest in a kind of art that broke all the rules. His friends included poet and playwright Federico García Lorca and filmmaker Luis Buñuel. Eventually, Dali was expelled from the school.

Whose Reality?

Dali painted in a very personal style. Objects in his paintings were as clear and detailed as in some photographs. But the objects themselves, and their settings, have a dreamlike quality. In one of his best-known works, *The Persistence of Memory,* metal watches seem to melt and drip onto the barren, endless landscape. It is as if time itself has ceased to exist.

Dali also liked to paint subjects that could be viewed two ways. An example of this technique is in *Apparition of Face and Fruit-Dish on a Beach,* which he painted in 1938. At the top of the painting is a seascape. A second look, however, reveals that the beach and bay form the head of a dog. In the same painting, a bowl of fruit also may be seen as a woman's forehead. The stem and base of the bowl become the woman's nose, mouth, and chin. Two seashells on the beach are her eyes. Which view is real, the artist asks.

In one of his most famous paintings—*The Persistence of Memory*—Dali created a haunting image of dead space and the end of time (watches melting or being devoured by insects).

Throughout his career, Dali actively sought attention and publicity. He is shown here immersed in water and sporting his trademark mustache.

Beyond the Canvas

Major Influence Dali did not limit his unique vision to painting. He also designed jewelry, ballet costumes, and stage sets. Many fashion designers and graphic artists were influenced by his work. In addition, Dali was sought after as a portrait painter. He and his wife Gala, who was his manager, often appeared in newspaper gossip columns. He adored the publicity and once declared himself "the only living genius."

Life in a Museum During much of his career, Dali divided his time between New York and Paris. In 1948, he returned to Spain and joined the Roman Catholic Church. His work became increasingly mystical and based on religious themes. He lived in a tower, which he had converted into a museum. Toward the end of his life, he rarely left the tower.

Salvador Dali died in 1989. While many art experts praised his technical skill, others criticized him for wasting his talent on short-lived artistic fads. Yet his disturbing, dreamlike images continue to attract attention and fascinate viewers.

Sometimes, Dali left his art to chance. In *Return of Ulysses,* he began by making inkblots on the paper. The gray and black blotches look as if they might be rocks along a coastline. Dali then used a brush and pen to draw a boat and figures on the shore. The "inkblot" technique had been developed by an 18th-century artist named Alexander Cozens. Dali's contemporary and fellow Surrealist Max Ernst also experimented with a similar technique.

Art for Fame's Sake Even as a young art student, Dali was considered eccentric. He enjoyed being the center of attention. He often dressed in a long, black cape or some other unusual garb. He once gave a lecture wearing a deep-sea diver's wet suit and a large metal helmet in which he nearly suffocated. For most of his life, he wore a long, thin mustache, which he waxed so it curled up at the ends.

Other Surrealists accused Dali of being more interested in promoting himself than in creating serious art. Some art critics believe that Dali painted his best works before he was 35. After that time, he seemed to focus his energy more on publicity and increasing his fortune. In 1936, at the peak of his career, Dali appeared on the cover of *Time* magazine. By 1939, the Surrealists—including Breton, Buñuel, and painter René Magritte—were fed up with Dali's public behavior and disassociated themselves from him. Dali, however, remained in the public eye.

This Dali painting, called *Morphological Echo,* is a study in repeated forms—ovals and arches. Morphological comes from the Greek word *morphē,* which means form or structure.

Glossary

abstract: Hard to understand. In art, abstract refers to works that have little or no resemblance to real objects.

aesthetics: The study of concepts of beauty, especially in art and literature.

Analytic Cubism: The most extreme phase of Cubism in which paintings resemble what a viewer might see if looking at an object through a prism.

avant-garde: A French term used to describe innovators, or those who use new techniques in their fields.

Baroque: An artistic style of the 16th and 17th centuries characterized by curved forms and lavish decoration.

Bauhaus: A German school of art founded in 1919 that stressed the use of science and technology. In architecture, it was thought that buildings should be simple and functional, with clean lines and little decoration.

Blue Period: An early period in Pablo Picasso's career (1901–1904), when his paintings were done primarily in shades of blue reflecting his feelings of sadness and alienation.

bronze: A reddish-brown metal that is a mixture of copper and tin.

cast: To fill a plaster mold with liquid bronze to create a statue.

ceramic: A product, such as brick or earthenware, made from a nonmetallic mineral that is heated to a high temperature.

chiaroscuro: The use of light and shadow to show three-dimensional forms.

Classical: Pertaining to the art and culture of ancient Greece and Rome. Classical art stressed certain established standards of form, such as balance, serenity, judgment, simplicity, and the treatment of mythological themes.

collage: A composition made by pasting various materials (such as paper, fabrics, wire, and photographs) onto a flat surface.

Collage Cubism: A style of Cubism created by attaching real objects, such as chair caning or newspaper clippings, to canvas.

commission: A formal order given to an artist requesting that something specific be made, such as a portrait or a sculpture.

conservative: Favoring a policy of conserving or keeping things the way they are; in art, favoring established styles and standards.

Cubism: An artistic style in which the subject is broken apart and reassembled by the artist in an abstract form, usually with geometric shapes.

daguerreotype: An early photograph produced on a metal plate, named after its inventor, L. J. M. Daguerre.

découpées: Colorful paper cutouts applied to a plain background.

engrave: To etch letters or designs on a surface, such as a metal plate or a wooden block, for printing.

etching: A print made from a metal plate on which a design has been scratched into wax and then eaten away by acid.

ethnography: The study of different cultures.

Expressionism: An artistic style in which the artist depicts personal responses to objects and events.

Fauvism: An artistic style characterized by the use of vivid colors and the free treatment of form.

fresco: A painting done with watercolors on wet plaster. The pigments, when mixed with the water, become chemically bound to the plaster.

Impressionism: An artistic style originating in France in the late 19th century. Shapes were only suggested, relying on each individual viewer's eye to interpret them.

Industrial Revolution: A change in social and economic organization that took place in the 18th and 19th centuries. A host of new inventions brought people from farms to cities to work in growing manufacturing industries.

International Style: A style of design developed and created at the Bauhaus in Germany, which combined architecture and modern technology.

mobile: A sculpture that moves by the force of wind or a motor.

mold: A detailed model, usually made from clay, which is filled with liquid bronze to create a piece of sculpture.

movable type: A printing method in which small blocks of type, such as a single letter, were assembled in a form and then inked. Paper was pressed against the inked type. The blocks of type could be taken apart and reassembled. By using movable type, multiple copies of a book could be printed in a short time. Before movable type, copies had to be made by hand or by using individual blocks one at a time.

mural: A picture, usually a large one, painted directly on a wall or a ceiling.

Neoclassical: Relating to the movement in art and architecture in the 17th and 18th centuries that revived or adapted the Classical style.

pre-Columbian: Any period in the Western Hemisphere before the arrival of Christopher Columbus.

primitive: Relating to art produced by the earliest societies. In Western art, primitive relates to artists who deliberately work in a simple, unsophisticated style.

radical: Marking a sharp departure from traditional or accepted views; proposing extreme changes in habits, conditions, institutions, or politics.

rationalism: The guiding of a person's actions and opinions based on what seems reasonable.

Realism: A mid-19th-century artistic style that pictured people and objects as they are in real life.

Reformation: A religious movement begun by Martin Luther in 1517 that created religious and political turmoil and led to the establishment of Protestant churches.

Renaissance: The revival of art, literature, and the sciences in Europe that began in the 14th century. The Renaissance was the transition period from the medieval world to the modern world. The name is from the French word for "rebirth."

Romanticism: An 18th-century artistic style that favored imagination, emotion, and nature as the most powerful forces, not human intelligence.

Rose Period: Period in Pablo Picasso's career (1904–1906) marked by paintings of clowns, jugglers, and circus scenes done in shades of red. It marked a more optimistic period in the artist's life after the Blue Period.

sfumato: A smokelike haziness that blurs or softens the edges of objects in a painting.

social commentary: Comments made and beliefs expressed by a person on some social or political issue. Artists, such as Pablo Picasso and Francisco Goya, often protested social conditions through their art by depicting controversial events and the suffering of the common people.

sociology: The study of society, social institutions, and human relationships.

stabile: An abstract sculpture that resembles a mobile but does not move.

subconscious: The mental processes of which an individual is unaware or only slightly aware.

Surrealism: An artistic movement where creativity was believed to come directly from the subconscious. Unnatural combinations were usual in Surrealist art.

tonal scale: A scale for measuring the gradation of tone in a black-and-white photograph. In between black and white are varying tones of gray, which enable a photographer to achieve contrast in a photograph.

woodcut: A print made from a block of wood on which the area not intended to carry ink has been cut away.

Suggested Readings

Note: An asterisk (*) denotes a Young Adult title.

Alinder, M. S. *Ansel Adams.* Bullfinch, 1990.

*Arenas, José Fernandez. *The Key to Renaissance Art.* Lerner, 1990.

*Bracons, José. *The Key to Gothic Art.* Lerner, 1990.

*Cirlot, Lourdes. *The Key to Modern Art of the Early 20th Century.* Lerner, 1990.

*Cockroft, James. *Diego Rivera.* Chelsea House, 1991.

*Corbishley, Mike. *The Middle Ages: Cultural Atlas for Young People.* Facts on File, 1990.

*Crisp, George. *Salvador Dali.* Chelsea House, 1994.

*Cumming, David. *Photography.* Raintree Steck-Vaughn, 1990.

Fine, Elsa H. *Women and Art: A History of Women Painters and Sculptors from the Renaissance to the 20th Century.* Westview, 1991.

Gowing, Lawrence. *Matisse.* Thames & Hudson, 1992.

*Haberman, Arthur, and Hundey, Ian. *Civilizations: A Cultural Atlas.* Gage, 1994.

Harris, Ann Sutherland, and Nocklin, Linda. *Women Artists: 1550–1950.* Knopf, 1977.

Herrera, Hayden. *Frida Kahlo: The Paintings.* HarperCollins, 1991.

*Hoobler, Dorothy, and Hoobler, Thomas. *Italian Portraits.* Raintree Steck-Vaughn, 1992.

Jacobus, John. *Matisse.* Abrams, 1983.

*Janson, H. W., and Janson, Anthony F. *History of Art for Young People.* 3rd ed. Abrams, 1987.

*Macauley, David. *Cathedral.* Houghton Mifflin, 1981.

Marshall, Norman F., and Rispamonti, Aldo. *Leonardo da Vinci.* Silver Burdett Press, 1990.

McLanathan, Richard. *Michelangelo.* Abrams, 1990.

Messinger, Lisa M. *Georgia O'Keeffe.* Thames & Hudson/Metropolitan Museum of Art, 1988.

Moore, Henry, and Hedgecoe, John. *Henry Moore: My Ideas, Inspiration, and Life as an Artist.* Chronicle Books, 1986.

Olson, Roberta J. *Italian Renaissance Sculpture.* Thames & Hudson, 1992.

Pinet, Helen. *Rodin: The Hands of Genius.* Abrams, 1992.

*Powell, Jillian. *Painting and Sculpture.* Raintree Steck-Vaughn, 1990.

Rey, Jean Dominique. *Berthe Morisot.* Crown, 1982.

*Reyero, Carlos. *The Key to Art: From Romanticism to Impressionism.* Lerner, 1990.

*Schwartz, Gary. *Rembrandt.* Abrams, 1992.

Scribner, Charles, III. *Gianlorenzo Bernini.* Abrams, 1991.

*Sills, Leslie. *Visions: Stories About Women Artists.* Albert Whitman, 1993.

*Sommer, Robin L., and McDonald, Patricia A. *Pablo Picasso.* Silver Burdett Press, 1990.

*Sproccati, Sandro. *Guide to Art.* Abrams, 1991.

*Triado, Juan-Ramon. *The Key to Baroque Art.* Lerner, 1990.

Welton, Jude. *Monet.* Dorling Kindersley, 1993.

Whitford, Frank. *Bauhaus.* Thames & Hudson, 1984.

*Van Zandt, Eleanor. *Architecture.* Raintree Steck-Vaughn, 1990.

Index